FURTHER STUDIES IN A DYING CULTURE

AAKAR BOOKS CLASSICS

FURTHER STUDIES IN A DYING CULTURE

Christopher Caudwell

Edited and with a preface by
Edgell Rickword

AAKAR

FURTHER STUDIES IN A DYING CULTURE
Christopher Caudwell

First Aakar Edition 2017

ISBN 978-93-5002-516-1

Published by
AAKAR BOOKS
28 E Pocket IV, Mayur Vihar Phase I
Delhi 110 091, India
aakarbooks@gmail.com
www.aakarbooks.com

Printed at
Sapra Brother, Delhi 110 092

CONTENTS

PREFACE

FOR those who pick up a book by Christopher Caudwell for the first time it is necessary to say that in 1937, when a young man of 29, he met his death in action against General Franco's Moorish troops. It is necessary to state this, because one of the leading themes of these essays is the unity of thinking and doing, the nullity of either in isolation. Caudwell did not stand 'dreaming on the verge of strife,' nor did he plunge into struggle without thought. His was consciously a different species of activity. 'Philosophers have hitherto only interpreted the world in various ways. The point however is to change it.' And for this young Englishman in 1936, as for so many generous hearted men and women all over the globe, the focal point of world change was the war between the Spanish Government and the internationally aided rebels. The philosopher, the lover of knowledge, could not but turn soldier in a struggle in which the forces of enlightenment and of obscurantism were so starkly opposed.

A decade of intensive experience lay behind Caudwell when he made his fateful decision. Those were years in which the existence of crisis was brought home to all but the most butterfly-minded. On all sides theories were propounded to account for the fact that hungry men and empty factories existed alongside men whose unsatisfied elemental needs those factories and workless men could have supplied. Economics was promoted the queen of sciences, but so many rival factions contended for the throne that the man in the street cursed them all equally heartily, for their words brought neither parsnips nor butter.

Caudwell had certainly an insatiable intellectual curiosity, a consuming Faustian ambition to master all the sciences. But whatever one studied in those days, the course of events always dragged back the attention to the realisation of economics, the material reproduction of our means of existence, as the basis of social organisation. It is a measure of the fantastic existence to which our minds were, and perhaps are, fashioned that such a self-evident proposition should rouse deep resentment and stimulate a counter-polemic of mystification, of juggling with sonorous abstractions.

When the garish boom of the late 20's suddenly collapsed into slump, with its lengthening queues of unemployed, the respective merits of those who claimed oracular status became of more than academic interest: and for the first time in this country on a considerable scale, the students and the white-collar workers found themselves as helpless as the worker in industry. The paradox of modern society, the impoverishment brought about by the most stupendous technological achievement, thrust itself, however unwelcome there, even into the millionaire's Press. Whilst as a temporary measure of alleviation food and industrial crops were destroyed (to keep up prices) it was seriously suggested that the only permanent cure for the disease of over-production was a technological holiday; not only should no new labour-saving devices be introduced, but existing machine processes should be turned back to manual labour in order to absorb the unemployed. These and other whimsies of like character were propounded by the economic pundits, and have been recorded for our delectation in the witty and poetic fantasias of Eimar O'Duffy.

I recall this nightmare period for the information of those

too young to remember it themselves, who perhaps started life when rearmament orders had set the wheels turning again, and because this experience of the break-down of a culture started Caudwell out on his quest for the means of regenerating society.

In the frustrated and bewildered condition that then afflicted us, the revival of interest in Marxism, with its massive clarification of the issues, could not be long delayed. In England, alone among European countries, Marx had been relegated to the status of an eccentric, and his existence was not acknowledged at universities. Since his brief influence in the eighties his work had been kept alive by small groups of working men (mainly in South Wales and the Clyde) who clubbed together to buy his weighty tomes from Kerr of Chicago. Now, he was in the very air. A mighty State acknowledged his teachings as the basis of the radical reconstruction of her economy and culture. Marxism was a light that radiated hope through the gloom of Britain's depressed areas as well as to the impoverished peasants of the colonies. To stamp out every vestige of understanding of what Marx had taught became the prime maxim and declared intention of another powerful State.

And having grasped from Marx the clue to the contemporary labyrinth, Caudwell found that the other knowledge he had acquired now fell into due place and proportion. What had before been an accumulation, 'a monstrously detailed collection of facts,' now became capable of organisation, of vitality. The special progress within each sphere of knowledge, the 'closed worlds' of Caudwell's phrase, which is certainly possible even within a culture decaying as a whole, could now be related to a general movement of society. The very pains rending our communities were revealed to be not death agonies but birth pangs.

Caudwell was not of the type to be content with a few

simple generalisations. Having the clue, he set out to explore with its aid deeply into contemporary reality, as that reality was being continually extended. And it was clear to him that he could not do this as the contemplative philosopher, in secluded study. He became a member of the Communist party and played a full part in its organisational and educational routine. Naturally so, since the working class had the decisive part to play in liberating society from its intolerable contradictions, but could not bring this about by spontaneous revolt against its immediate deprivations.

The pressure of continual crisis, to which we have been subjected for a generation, induces a tendency to evasion, which is very noticeable in the behaviour pattern of to-day, particularly among the intellectuals. The perspective is more than the individual can bear to contemplate alone, and whereas faith is gregarious, the exercise of reason seems solitary. That is not how it was with Caudwell, who through reason came to achieve solidarity. I feel that his writings will be read to-day with even more understanding than when they were written, for the dozen years that have passed have immensely emphasised the world-pattern which he discerned, so that it is more easily visible than before. In no case, I think, has his position been falsified by events, for the technological advances necessitated by the late war have already exacerbated the conflicts and contradictions within the capitalist system, and this morbid condition finds its reflection in the violence and sensationalism which provide an increasing proportion of the subject-matter represented in literature and the film.

This book contains what were, it seems from internal evidence, Caudwell's latest writings and they show the developing originality and maturity of his mind. As a precaution lest some details of which he wrote in the essay 'Consciousness' should have been outmoded by subsequent research, I sent the manuscript to one of our younger neurologists: who replied that so far from this being the case, 'Caudwell brilliantly anticipates a whole trend which is now discernable in modern neuro-anatomy. The experimental material was not available when he was writing so that the value of his application of the Marxist method to the facts as then known is dramatically revealed by the results of subsequent investigation.'

Another comment on these essays was: 'Caudwell has the power of making his conceptual world very densely peopled, and what distinguishes him, in my opinion, is his extreme awareness of the different fields of consciousness and his ability to link them up.' The exposition of any theory tends to be thin, exclusive of all else, but Caudwell's writing is like an exciting discussion for he is always conscious of an invisible interlocutor, keen witted opponent of his own thesis. He had not merely grasped Marxism intellectually or emotionally; it had entered into the fabric of his life so that he thought in it, as one can think in a new language, not merely translate it into one's own. But the warmth of emotion, too, glows through the argument so that it becomes at times true eloquence. The essay on Aesthetics, the most abstruse of abstract subjects, reminds us that Caudwell had the creative as well as the ratiocinative gift, and that poetry and art were as essential to his sense of fitness as bread and air. And in the paragraph which forms the peroration to this book he has written his own apologia and sufficient epitaph.

Edgell Rickword

NOTE

The quotation from Marx which follows was placed by Caudwell at the head of one of his essays, but it is so essentially a statement of his starting point that it comes naturally as a prelude to the whole book.

Thanks are due to Dr. B. H. Kerman for his notes on the technical aspects of certain statements in the essay 'Consciousness.'

From Karl Marx:

INTRODUCTION TO THE CRITIQUE OF POLITICAL ECONOMY

'In the social production of their means of life, human beings enter into definite and necessary relations which are independent of their will: production relations which correspond to a definite stage in the development of their productive forces. The totality of these production relations constitutes the economic structure of society, the real basis upon which a legal and political superstructure arises, and to which definite forms of social consciousness correspond.

'The mode of production of the material means of life determines, in general, the social, political, and intellectual processes of life. It is not the consciousness of human beings which determines their existence, it is their social existence which determines their consciousness.

'At a certain stage of their development the material productive forces of society come into conflict with the existing production relationships. Or, what is a legal expression for the same thing, with the property relationships within which they have hitherto moved. From forms of development of the productive forces those relationships turn into fetters upon them. A period of social revolution then begins.

'With the change in the economic foundation the whole gigantic superstructure is more or less rapidly transformed. In considering such transformations we must always distinguish between the material changes in the economic conditions of production (changes which can be determined with the precision of natural science) and the legal, political, religious, aesthetic, or philosophic—in short ideological—

forms in which human beings become conscious of this conflict and fight it out to an issue.

'Just as little as we can judge an individual by what he thinks of himself, just so little can we appraise such a revolutionary epoch in accordance with its own consciousness of itself. On the contrary, we have to explain the consciousness as the outcome of the contradictions of material life, of the conflict existing between social productive forces and production relationships.

'No social order is destroyed until all the productive forces for which it gives scope have been developed: new and higher production relations cannot appear until the material conditions for their existence have ripened within the womb of the old social order. Therefore mankind in general never sets itself problems it cannot solve: since, looked at more closely, we always find that the problem arises only when the material conditions for its solution exist, or at least, are already in process of formation.

'We can in broad outline designate the Asiatic, the Classical, the Feudal, and the modern Bourgeois forms of production as progressive epochs in the economic formation of society.

'The bourgeois production relations are the final antagonistic form in the development of social production—antagonistic, not in the sense of an antagonism between individuals, but one inherent in the life conditions and social circumstances of the individuals, at the time when the productive forces developing in the womb of bourgeois society are creating the material conditions for the solution of that antagonism.

'This social formation, therefore, constitutes the closing chapter of the prehistoric stage of human society.'

I

THE BREATH OF DISCONTENT

A Study in Bourgeois Religion

IN the study of comparative religion, bourgeois scholarship has from time to time attempted to draw a distinction between magic and religion. The original distinction was theological; it took a subtler form when magic came to be regarded as the primitive parent of science, of the belief in the universal reign of causality. But lacking a definition of either magic or religion that was really analytical, bourgeois culture has never been able to produce a science of comparative religion which would be both explanatory and inclusive; it has always at some stage or other in the study revealed its own unscientific content.

Various psychological explanations of the evolution of religion have been put forward, of which Freud's *Totem and Tabu* is representative, in which well-known psychoanalytical mechanisms are called upon to explain the development of religion. But if man's psyche is genetically unchanging, the story of religion cannot be explained in terms of the individual psyche, for a most important characteristic of religion is just its wide variation, a variation out of all proportion to the trifling genetic variation of men in historic times. The study of religion, in any scientific sense, must therefore be the study of those causes, *independent of any individual psyche*, which produce in the individual psyche the religious beliefs and attitudes that we know from history.

Attempts have been made to explain the development of different religious beliefs from animism to Christianity, as the result of an evolutionary process in the course of which religion passes through a series of stages. Such a notion is only evolutionary in the abstract, for it deals with the evolution, not of objective religion but of the idea of religion. Religion exists as a sum of human beliefs and actions, of beliefs held by real individuals acting in a real society. Its evolution can therefore only be considered as part of the evolution of real men in real society. This so-called evolutionary school first abstracts religious beliefs from the men who hold and act them, and then studies their possible development. This is a logical, not a real, evolution. Since the material threads making the visual pattern—man's real active existence producing religious beliefs—have been cut, the submerged interconnection which would explain the pattern is no longer accessible.

Of all the bourgeois schools the most realistic in its approach is the 'functional' school of whose theory Malinowski and his pupil Audrey Richards are leading exponents. This school deals with the religious beliefs of primitives only as they evidence themselves in primitive life, not merely as abstract 'beliefs' but in action, as part of the warp and woof of daily social transactions.

But it is part of the doom of bourgeois culture that it can only achieve such correct approaches in closed worlds, in a limited sector. Although the functional method is formally correct, it gets applied only to a limited sphere—the study of certain primitive peoples—and the observers continually show the basic confusion of their views on the relations of men, nature and society. To be a thorough-going functionalist as regards Melanesian or Bantu society, would be to be a Marxist and a dialectical materialist.

The view of human society taken by this school is not

really functional, for it does not include, as functions of society, the 'civilised' equipment the observers themselves bring to their survey of primitive society. Thus even their primitive society is never more than a collection of individuals, for there is no real attempt to discern in the collection of individuals those relations which make it a society and are the seat of change and development. Society for them is static and non-historic, as if it were the result of a crystallation and not of an evolutionary movement.

Bourgeois culture has, however, not been content with three different ways of explaining the evolution of religion. There is also the environmental explanation, in which religious beliefs are the projection of natural phenomena (sun and rain and sky myths); the individualistic explanation, in which cunning priests, kings, and chiefs seize hold of man's 'natural' belief in magic to impose their rule and a settled cosmogony on their fellows; and the idealistic explanation, in which religion is due to the birth or evolution of the Ideas of Spirit, Goodness, Awe, and so on.

Marx, however, developing in his revolutionary activity Feuerbach's and Morgan's pioneer work, had shown nearly 100 years ago the correct path to follow—not as a new 'fad' derived from a limited sphere (the psycho-analytical, evolutionary, or functional approaches) but as part of a consistent world-view, the arrival at which meant that one had ceased to be bourgeois.

(i) 'Religion is a *fantastic reality*.' *

Fantastic, because the statements it makes about existents are incorrect, because the ideas of outer reality incorporated in it do not correspond with outer reality. *Real*, because

* The sentences on which Caudwell comments in the next few pages are quoted from a famous passage in Marx's *Introduction to a Critique of Hegel's Philosophy of Law*, given in full at the end of this essay, page 75 (Ed.)

these ideas are causally linked with material reality, and are not only determined but also determine, in their turn exerting a causal influence on their matrix. Thus by acknowledging that religious ideas are not spontaneous but form part of active reality, Marxism is able to analyse more deeply the real causes which produced them. The analysis of religion becomes also an analysis of society.

(ii) 'Religion is consciousness of self and the self-feeling of a man who has not yet found himself or has lost himself again.'

The animals are not religious, and religion thus becomes a badge of man, not as mere animal but as distinct from animals, and man distinct from animals is man in association as a functioning group, a group engaged in economic production. Religion is seen to be, like the consciousness of which it is a part, an economic product. Because it is conscious it is 'higher' than the blind unconscious knowledge of reality shown by the animal in its actions, the animal whose 'notions' of causality exist implicitly as mere conditioned or unconditioned reflexes. Yet religion is a *distorted* knowledge of reality. It is a consciousness of self which is lawless and unattached—which has not yet found itself or has lost itself. Such a man is conscious of himself, but projects this consciousness outside himself, unaware as yet of his own necessities or of the universe of causality in which his existence is grounded.

(iii) 'Man is not an abstract being existing outside the world. Man—that is the world of men, the State, society.'

This consciousness is not the consciousness of an abstract average man. It is the self-feeling of a man in the world of men, living in active social relations with other men, and forming a distinctive society. It is the self-feeling of a particular individual in a particular society at a particular time, and hence the study of religion is inseparable from the study of society.

(iv) 'This state, this society, produces religion—an inverted consciousness of the world—because the world is itself an inverted world.'

The religious distortion of consciousness is produced by the structure of the society in which it is generated. It is the outcome of an illusion, a flaw, an infection, in that society. Thus the criticism of religion is also the criticism of the society that produced it, and this does not mean a criticism of that society in the abstract but of its concrete reality, a criticism of all the social relations engendered by its level of economic production.

(v) 'The struggle against religion is therefore, indirectly, the struggle against that world whose spiritual aroma is religion.'

Since the criticism of religion becomes, to Marxism, the criticism of the concrete social relations which produced it, the struggle against its errors and its distortions can never be a struggle against religion as such—a kind of armchair atheism—because such a struggle is not a real one—it is ideal truth fighting ideal religion and both, when abstracted from action, are unreal. The very criticism of religion, as soon as it becomes criticism of concrete religion, becomes criticism of the social relations that engendered it, and when this criticism emerges creatively as a struggle, it will not be an ideal struggle against religious ideas but a concrete struggle against real social relations. There is no absolute tvuth to set against fantastic lies, but fantastic reality whose fantastic content is exposed in real living.

(vi) 'Religious misery is at once the expression of real *misery* and a protest against that *real* misery. Religion is the sigh of the hard-pressed creature ; the heart of a heartless world . . . It is the opium of the people.'

But what we have previously said does not mean that the struggle against religion is merely the struggle against the non-religious social relations that produced it, and that religion is exempted from the field of battle. The struggle is against the real, concrete, social relations which produce these beliefs, and some of these relations are religious relations. The whole of concrete society is the domain of Marxism, and religion is included in concrete society now. The religious beliefs, and those social forms that are religious, are part of the existing superstructure of society. Active criticism of that society involves the transformation of its social relations, and therefore encounters the resistance of all those men for whom the superstructure is the expression of their special status and privilege in society. This resistance makes use of all the forms of the existing superstructure, including the religious forms. Religious beliefs are part of the form in which 'men become conscious of the struggle and fight it out to an issue.'

Yet religion is 'at once the expression of real *misery* and a protest against that *real* misery.' It pictures an inverted world which, just because it is inverted, will also be a criticism of the real world. A religion expressive of the social relations of a virile and active age may, as those relations emerge more and more clearly as the bulwark of an exploiting class now grown parasitic, finally find some of its content in antagonism to that exploiting class. Conversely the religion which embodies the protest of an exploited class may, as that class becomes revolutionary and creative, itself grow vital and insurgent. Religion, because it is the opium of the people and not the pride of the exploiting class, may at some stage give rise to a revolutionary religion, the weapon of the people.

*　　　*　　　*

Is magic then a 'human weakness' and religion a specific

social product, its form and role only varying according to the society in which it is found? Marx was able to answer these questions in the course of his sociological analysis:—

Magic is the product of a primitive society. (Man's self-feeling before he has found himself). Religion is the product of a class society. (Man's self-feeling when he has lost himself). Dialectical materialism is the product of a classless society. (Man's self-feeling when he has found himself again).

'The primitive man may recognise the sensations he experiences without an adequate knowledge of their causes. Malinowski states that the Trobriand Islanders enjoy the act of eating without any knowledge of the physiological function of nutrition, just as they enjoy sexual pleasure without being aware of the physiological nature of paternity. This was not so with the natives among whom I worked, but I noticed that the sensations connected with the alimentary or sexual functions were reckoned on a par with what we should describe as emotional conditions—such as anger or sorrow. It must be remembered here that visceral sensations actually are produced through the action of the involuntary nervous system under the strain of strong emotions such as fear or rage. The savage recognises that eating, sexual satisfaction, pregnancy, as well as a number of emotions, may all be responsible for physiological sensations which are, in many respects, similar. What wonder that he concludes sometimes that their cause is similar? 'When I drink beer I feel hot inside, as I do when I am angry,' a Muhemba said to me; and a man who has just had sexual intercouse is also described as 'hot.' Radcliffe-Brown points out that the word *kimil* is used by the Andaman Islander to describe heat, the condition of a man after eating and also after slaying an enemy. It is well known, too, that among some primitive tribes pregnancy is supposed to be a result of eating some special food recognised by the first attack of sickness that the woman experiences. The Malayan speaks of the *hantu* or the spirit of the forest, together with the *hantu* that makes people gamble, smoke opium, dispute, or those that produce stomach-ache or headache, as though all these could be traced to a similar cause. In fact, as Mr. Smith sums up the situation among the Ba-ila: 'The parts they assign to the organs in the economy of the body are psychical rather than physiological, i.e. they regard them more as the seats of emotion than of vital processes.'*

Are animals ignorant of causality? In so far as they are able to respond actively and correctly to stimuli (leaping on a moving object, turning towards a sound) they prove their knowledge of causality. They show a conditioned reflex, in which the conditioning represents a certain knowledge of causality acquired from experience. But it is unconscious knowledge.

With the evolution of primitive man self-consciousness emerges. It emerges as an affect, as a feeling which is not merely the glow of action but something which can be recalled, can become the object of perception, and can be externalised. It can be described.

But it is the self-feeling of a man who has yet not found himself. The affect awakened by the stimulus appears to lead a violent, solitary life of its own. It is common to a range of actions and is yet distinguishable from them. On the one hand it is separate, an ego, a stable power; on the other hand it interpenetrates reality, attaching itself to a variety of active, interesting movements in outer reality. And because it attaches to reality, it begins to take on itself some of the attributes and interest of outer reality. The fear becomes the thing feared; the desire, the thing desired: the feeling of domination the *actual* domination of reality. The affect is plastic and fluid as reality is not. It is movable, recallable, shareable; it is a substitute for reality. It is the self-feeling of the man who has not found himself, because

* Audrey I. Richards. *Hunger and Work in a Savage Tribe*, 1932

he has not yet come to regard himself as part of reality, in causal unity with it. How could he do so, when the first stage of consciousness was the separation of himself from reality—the discrimination of subject from object as a struggle, as an antagonism of self against not-self?

Consciousness emerges then as a 'lost,' bewildered affect, apparently full of illusion and fluidity. It is precisely this fluidity which gives it its value and ultimately its justification as the vehicle of higher truths.

The affect, which emerges in the individual as a common reaction to a variety of experiences, becomes the gesture and finally the word which, because it is external and similar, becomes for the group a social name crystallising the common adventures of the group in the world of reality. Because the affect involves or is rooted in a similar behaviour it becomes the means, *via* the word, of organising social behaviour in reference to the varying phenomena of the outside world. Each enriches the other, and language and consciousness grow as a result of their interaction with a continually elaborating universe.

It is this interaction which is social and tribal. Nutrition and shelter and protection from wild beasts involve a series of elaborate actions performed in unison and by no means instinctive—in short, economic production. Such elaborate activities can only be co-ordinated by an elaboration of affect and word organisations which thus contain within their interstices a *social* view of outer *reality* and a *community* of emotionally tinged *ideas*. Thus any picture of the individual consciousness at the start detaching itself as a simple ego from all reality, and acquiring its own presentations and organising them, is false; for consciousness emerges as the concomitant of economic production, as part and parcel of man's interpenetration with outer reality. That interpenetration generates consciousness, which is therefore full of the impress of both. The formation of consciousness is an active process, now and historically; but because the activity is social and secured by a division of labour, this is not obvious to introspection.

What then is the part that magic plays in this active interpenetration? It is seen everywhere to be the activity of primitive or atavistic man who, having become conscious of himself, attempts to find himself by projecting his self-feeling into outer reality, in the form of spirits, (animism), forces, demons, hantu, djinns, nymphs, genii, powers, mana, ghosts, devils. And he projects, not only the affects but the active organisation of them, so that it seems possible to control reality by those movements which have accompanied such affects in the past. Rain-making, harvest, the multiplication of food-animals and the like, is secured by imitating the noise of the rain, the actions of sowing or reaping the harvest, and the gait or appearance of the animals.

By thus projecting his self-feeling into outer reality, man also feels *his* way into it. True, he makes the environmental *human*, arbitrary, emotional. But as a result he also makes *himself* environmental. He comes from the transaction enriched with a knowledge of reality.

He makes as it were a series of magic propositions about reality, a chain of wish-fulfilments. In acting according to these, he imperceptibly finds imposed on them, by interaction with reality, a real structure, a determined pattern. As a result of experience, his prayers for rain are made at the beginning of the rainy season, his fertility rites are performed in spring. He prays to the sun to rise at dawn, and does not ask it to rise immediately after it has set. The inhabitants of desert lands do not pray for rain. Thus all his self-feeling, projected into outer reality, is organised by it, and what were at first all-powerful emotions, apparently dominating reality, became words emotionally charged, and yet organised and 'influenced' by reality, and, finally those become symbols (mathematics) which are like a transparent dress conforming to the shape of outer reality. All this has been achieved by his active interpenetration with reality. (Newtonian 'forces' of gravity still retain a colouring of magic, but already the medium is almost colourless.)

In doing so man has also become conscious of 'himself'. He sees his body as a part of the environment; as subject to the same laws. He sees parts of his body, no longer as seats of emotions, but as seats of physiological functions. He sees himself as part of the determined unity of reality. He becomes not merely conscious *as* a self, but conscious *of* himself. He, the subject, becomes to himself an object.

He sees this determined unity as a changing unity of opposites, and himself as an active opposite, realising his affects, not blindly and unknowingly but according to the necessities of the Universe. He has become conscious of necessity, and therefore of all reality.

The fluidity of the affects remains. The affects are attached to ideas, and his ideas therefore remain fluid, but he does not now suppose that in organising his ideas according to his affective drives he is altering reality. He is only altering himself. That is to say he has ceased to create mythologies, creeds, schemes of salvation and theologies, and become an artist, aware that his story, picture, or sound-group is not a reflex of actual reality (as the priests maintain) but an art work. Or, if the ideas rather than the affects are his main interest in this shuffling, he knows he is not altering reality, but experimenting with possible changes as a scientist and putting forward hypotheses.

Man, then, has completely found himself. This is not the end only of man's prehistoric stage. This inaugurates the most eventful age of man. It is precisely art and science that are more fluid and evolutionary than magic and religion. When magic and religion end, therefore, the prehistoric stage of man's evolution ends, and he has at last completely found himself. He has become conscious, not only of outer reality but of himself, as part with it of the one active process.

* * *

And then, too, he has necessarily become conscious of society. We have so far stated the interpenetration in terms of one average man and nature, but this interpenetration is only the outcome of the increase in complexity of society, and thus when man is finally in a position to become conscious of the complete, active, subject-object relation, a whole fabric of social being has been built up, a complex and rich organism, of which he must now become conscious in order to achieve the final integration.

It is just because the interpenetration is the result of a social economic process, handling real matter, real nature and real men, that it is not a simple ideal movement, but slowly and painfully developed. It is because consciousness is the product of social life that magic and religion have the complex elaborate history they do have. It is because of the laws of social relations, of which man is until the end unconscious, that man seems to find himself and lose himself again and again. This is because at the best he only finds himself as he is not, in the way he finds himself in Aristotle, Plato, Lucretius, Plotinus, Ockham, Aquinas, Hobbes, Helvetius, Kant, and Hegel; he finds himself as an individual in civil society. He is not this. This conception shuts off from his self-knowledge huge areas of himself, and drives him to and fro from one contradiction to another. He finds himself fully and finally only as more than an individual in civil society, as an individual *because* of civil society, as a node in the social plexus.

Sub-man must have been formed into society and humanity as the result of a process which forced on him economic production. By economic production we mean an active interpenetration of organism with nature that is not innate, is not genetically inherited, but is transmitted by external means, and yet is not environmental in the biological sense. It is cultural.

It is therefore almost a tautology to say that economic production is what makes man man, for any real definition of it at once delimits as a distinct sphere all the human qualities, and at the same time exhibits those qualities as social, as the result of man being in economic production *associated man*. Speech, ideas, reason, art, consciousness, writing tools, truth, morality, law, ethics and ideals—all these are seen to emerge as social and not individual properties. Though present in the individual they are generated as a social process and seem external.

The attempt to control nature in a new way is therefore forced on man by nature, and given in the very form of the attempt is society—the non-genetical inheritance of an active interpenetration of man and nature. This proves itself a richer and more powerful method than the biological interpenetration. The struggle becomes more acute; the war between man and nature is waged on more and more fronts; and it is precisely this undying hostility, this furious antagonism, which produces a greater humanisation of the environment by man and a greater environmentalisation of man by nature.

Having gathered itself apart from nature as something separate and antagonistic, man's self-feeling or consciousness is simultaneously projected on to nature. *This itself is the reflex of man's greater separation from nature by economic production and the increasing humanisation of nature (huts, tilled land, tamed animals) which that interpenetration produces.*

Therefore in the world of magic, it seems as if man's self-feeling was an active creative force, and that the emotions he felt stir within him were flooding the world of reality. They seem to possess *him* (for he has not yet found himself) and nature, (for he is in active relation with nature) and to be sources of movement and power, moulding the world of phenomena to their shape. The world therefore becomes interpreted in terms of these affects, but since affects cannot be bodied forth socially and interpretation is a social action, these affects become interpreted in terms of the stock of ideas socially available, drawn from the social activity of the community, and in terms of the actions and behaviour of men in society. This very interpretation changes them, and we have therefore a mythology in which ordinary terms, the description of ordinary activities, and ordinary men, women, and animals become large, sacred, rigid, hieratic, awesome and hybrid. We have a series of actions which become formalised, stereotyped, emotional and abstract—the ritual dances, ceremonies and initiations. This body of magic ideas and behaviour acts and reacts upon profane ideas and behaviour but in a primitive community never becomes isolated from them. Most activities and ideas have a magical element; most magical activities have a social function.

Now because such a magic is the by-product of the social relations engendered by economic production, it advances and develops equally with production at the primitive level of society. Economic production is realising magic's promises. In magic the primitive's desires become detached as beneficent or evil spirits with power to change and mould reality to their will. This is precisely what economic production does—it humanises the environment. Man's desire for plenty, externalised as the god plenty, does through economic production make the wilderness blossom and hunting prosper.

Magic presupposes a vast power not actually realised by primitive economic production. Admittedly, but economic production at the bourgeois level will give man powers undreamed of by the primitives, and then, precisely because the intemperate desires of magic are at last 'realised', made real (and *changed* in thus becoming concrete), magic itself will disappear, having been sucked into reality. Until then magic, though generated by economic production, is in antagonism to it, and this antagonism, by reaching always beyond man's powers now, drives him on in hope and confidence to new levels of production.

This process also acts as a kind of channel for magic, and gives it its characteristic shape. It produces a distinction between 'black' and 'white' magic. 'White' magic is social magic; it is magic rooted in economic production. It is magic which does not, for example, demand manna in the desert, or sit back and ask the gods to reap and sow the fields or Robin Goodfellow to make the butter. It is magic which 'asks the blessing of the gods', or 'brings mana,' force, magic power upon all the social activities concerned in economic production. It asks this power and this blessing upon the arduous labour of the harvest, the hopeful spring sowing, the making of canoes and of huts, the driving of animals, the various crises associated with the development of such economic units as the family, the class, or the clan—marriage, birth, initiation and death. This magic is not a substitute for such economic production. It does not ask the gods to ripen the grains at once, or demand of magic in this world immortal life. It is a relish to economic production. It asks the gods to put heart and luck into the labour. By holding out the divine certainty of harvest, or the promise of children, or the magic enforcement of game, it gives man courage and heart for the lengthy labours required before his satisfaction. It does this by the dance, the chant, the fable and myth, the feast in common.

Since the gods and the forces which man has projected by magic into nature are mere embodiments and reflections of his own self-feeling, and since the purpose of magic ceremonies is simply to awaken such emotions in his heart, there is a reality in magic. The gods, which were originally personal emotions projected into nature in social clothes, become in magic ceremonies stripped of their clothes, and return again into the heart as bare emotions, but now changed by their intervening life. They are taken out of the social cold storage of mythology. The god comes again into the worshipper; the worshipper is said to become the god, as in Dionysian rites—and truly, for the god was never more than the social crystallisation of the affects of a number of worshippers, which now return into them simultaneously.

Though magic is a reality, it is a *fantastic* reality. Affects and outer reality are blended, and confusingly blended. One distorts the other; man has not yet learned to distinguish them in science and art. Yet the very interpenetration which begets their distortion also ensures at this stage their mutual correction. Magic does not replace economic production: it is a special offshoot of it, and therefore is a distorted reflection of it. But it is a conscious, cultural reflection, portable, easily inherited and easily modified. These conveniences outweigh the distortions. Because magic, by reason of its association with economic production, contains in its mythology and ritual the correct operations for sowing and reaping or hunting, crystallises the family and tribal social relations, is a compendious calendar and tribal guide, and can be handed on and shared socially, it is an invaluable ally to economic production. It is a special social consciousness of economic production, of the functioning of the tribe in relation to nature.

It is thus parent of science. In proportion as economic production develops and becomes a division of labour, magic splits up and soon ceases to reflect man's direct relation to nature. It ceases to be an almanac and storehouse of the more abstract and generalised economic experiences. It becomes on the one hand art, in which all its affective organisation crystallises, and on the other hand science, in which all its cognitive organisation is marshalled. Thus with the development of art and science magic as an important vital element in economic production disappears, because the very development of economic production which it has helped to bring about has made it unnecessary. Man has found himself. He has separated himself from the environment again, in art and science, not absolutely but as part of a new and more active interpenetration. Magic now only survives, not as the proud flower of social life, mother of all social power and status, but as something lingering on in interstices and crevices.

Even while the development of science and art reveals more truly the precise relation between man and nature, between man's self-feeling and nature's necessity, a relation which magic only imperfectly expressed, the division of labour in economic production had provided a development in magic. The two developments overlapped. Magic disappeared, became outcast and suspect, became increasingly replaced by science and art, and at the same time magic re-appeared in a new and more powerful form. It became religion.

* * *

In fact of course religion was always latent in magic. We call it religion only when it shows an organisation, a coherence, a tough, visible structure. This organisation, coherence and structure are themselves only possible as the result of the development of economic production, through the division of labour, to a level where society becomes complex and highly organised. The development of classes in society makes magic into religion, and gives religion a characteristic form reflecting the class structure in turn, as the form of a specific level of economic production. Even at the earliest level of economic production, religion is visible in men's religious attitude towards the dead. The dead and the not-dead are the two great divisions of primitive society which seem almost to stand to each other in the relation of exploited to exploiting classes. The living owe their productive level to the capital, the instruments of production, the instruction, the wisdom, and the transmitted culture of the dead who therefore continue to live in the interstices of the society they have departed from in body. This half-life of the dead, constantly recalled to the living by their instructions, their leavings and their social formulations, is the other-world survival of the dead in all primitive societies which, as the researches of anthropologists increasingly show, is probably the most important element in primitive religious beliefs. This immortality of the dead is a fantastic reality. The dead really live on socially in the inherited culture of society, but to the primitive they live fantastically, clothed in the affective and concrete images of his dreams in another, ghostly world.

Just as magic expressed man's confused perception of the relation of man's self-feeling to nature's necessities, and disappears when man finds himself in a true relation to nature in science and art, so religion expresses man's confused perception of the relation of man's self-feeling to society's necessities, and disappears when man completely finds himself in society. Until then, religion seems separate from magic, and seems to tower above science and art, for science and art are still distorted and confused by the confusion of man's self-feeling, and have not yet realised themselves in society. Religion expresses—and therefore defends—a class-confused society, a society whose view of itself is only a fantastic reality because its economic production still functions within the limits imposed by a ruling class. The struggle against religion, unlike the struggle against magic, is therefore a struggle against class. The struggle of one religion against another is the struggle of one class against another, and the struggle against all religion can only be realised as the struggle for a classless society. Only when conditions are ripe for the creation of such a society, therefore, can the struggle against religion be the important turning-point of ideological activity.

Just as magic is a confused perception of man's relation to reality, but, in spite of its confusion, proves more valuable and more powerful than the unconsciousness of beasts, because it is a conscious perception and therefore a *social* perception, so religion, although a confused perception of man's relation to society, is more valuable than no perception of social relations at all. Indeed it is essential to the early development of 'civilised' society. As long as economic production remains below the point at which classes can vanish, so long the evolution of religion merely expresses the struggle between different forms of class societies. All those social relations in which production relations emerge to consciousness disguised and veiled, are social relations which inevitably include religion.

In primitive societies, where division of labour is hardly practised, social relations have not developed such complexity that a bewildering superstructure is interposed between man and the basis of his life, his struggle with nature. Man finds himself in association with others directly confronted by nature. In this fight magic is the heartener, the confused symbol of man's powers, the affect broken loose and humanising the environment. In so far as it is secreted by this struggle and regularised by participation in economic production, magic is also to the tribe the textbook manual and educator in the technique of association for economic production. It thus *is* reality, although a fantastic reality. Archaeology finds all men's first formulations of causality—the calendar, cosmogony, and physiology—and of affective realities—art, dance, tragedy—and of social relations—the family, the class, the tribe—emerge first in a magical dress.

Magic can also be used independently of man associated in economic production. These magical affects, made detached and plastic by the rituals of the tribe, can be used by the individual against other individuals. The word, which is a social creation and derives its power as a tool from its social role, can be harnessed in private spells and chants to private ends—against personal enemies or for personal goods.

Now it is not possible for such magic to add to the tribe's knowledge because it is not secreted in the process of economic production and therefore is not pressed against the shape of reality. It is not a science in embyro. It cannot be tested out in practice by society, and so rectified. It is private, whispered, individualistic. It is not deeply intertwined with outer reality, like public magic, by partaking of economic production. It is not transmitted as a body of experience for tribal use. It is therefore a degeneration—the use of tribal capital for personal aims. Society made magic, for it made the common word and gesture which seem to possess a power beyond the individual. It does possess a power beyond the individual, it possesses the power of associated men, which is composed of and yet external to individuals, which is not innate but leads a strange life of its own and is fitly symbolised in the form of ghosts and forces. This social power the wizard uses for individual ends. Black magic or witchcraft as opposed to white magic or ritual is therefore rightly condemned as anti-social, disruptive and dangerous. It is wicked, just as white magic is holy—'Thou shalt not suffer a witch to live.' Because it is unconventional and does not use socially recognised forms embodying the structure of society as its channel, it is opposed to white magic and religion. Thus all innovators in religion will be met by religion with the cry of 'witches,' 'heretics,' 'wicked men,' because they negate the social norms of the time. All such negation seems wicked. The question is whether they are rebels and revolutionaries expressing new productive forces struggling for release or merely maladapted individuals making anti-social sorties. If they are harbingers of a successful revolution, they in their turn will become holy.

Magic remains at the level of magic only in a primitive society. In such a society, economic production knows no division of labour except that arising from genotypical as distinct from imposed classes. Such classes are formed by the sexes, which in turn may be divided into children, initiated, adolescents, bachelors, married, and aged. Such a primitive society is best seen in Australia, but is common to all tribes still at the food-gathering stage of culture.

When economic production passes beyond food-gathering to settled agriculture, a division of labour takes place which involves in each unit a man who acts as director of labours, keeper of the calendar, custodian of the social capital in the form of seeds, implements, or garnered fruits. This is the village headman, who becomes the chief, and, as agriculture develops to the stage where it requires perhaps irrigation works, huge granaries, and the creation of roads and canals he becomes the god-king, ending as the apex of the pyramid of subordinate or autonomous directors of operations—priests, lords, mandarins and the like. When agriculture has passed from gardening to grain growing, he emerges as the Pharaoh of Egypt, the kings of Babylon and the Mesopotamian city states, the Emperor of China, the Mikado of Japan. His exact position and his relation to similar exalted personages depend on the development of economic production, which in turn will depend upon the topography and climate of the area, its relation with other areas, its own past history, and the internal forces produced by the development of the superstructure.

Such a man derives his magic power not, as Frazer imagines, from his cunning in imposing himself as a magician on his 'naturally' credulous neighbours but because his role, forced on him by the division of labour, makes him in fact custodian of those supra-individual forces which arise from division of labour and the association of men. Such division and association does wield powers which are more than the individual himself can wield in the struggle against nature. As long as his perception of the origin of these forces remains confused, the individual feels that they are external to him and more powerful than him. He therefore abases himself to these forces. Since these forces are plainly wielded by the king or chief, they seem concentrated in the person of the chief or king, who therefore seems awful, holy, sacred, all-powerful and divine. The precise relation of this chief to the symbols in which the magical consciousness of the tribe has bodied forth its social affects, depends on a chain of historical circumstances, which in no case follow exactly the same route. The relationship between the chief and the animal or human personifications of these social forces, is always close. The chief is the incarnation or son or favoured instrument of such forces. The god converses with him or dwells in him.

The family is the economic unit of primitive society: the medium by which food—which does not come on a market—is distributed and by which the inherited capital of the tribe in the form of technique, language and the memorised plexus of social relations, is transmitted to the babe. It is the primary educational unit of the tribe, becoming increasingly important with the increase in size of the tribe, which forces the family to take over many clan functions. Such an increase in size can only take place as the result of the development of economic production. Thus the god-king or holy chief comes into being at the same time as the family unit becomes of increased importance as the main economic channel. In the chief's family his children will learn the rudiments of his special task and be themselves therefore specially qualified to perform it. Thus a unique virtue will seem to inhere in the blood royal: the sacredness of kingship, derived from direction of the community's labour power, will seem hereditary. A ruling class will have completely emerged, whose power and prerogatives, because of the confused nature of man's perception of society and his deficient powers of abstraction, will seem to be inherent in and arise from the chief's blood.

The division of labour in agriculture, because of its efficiency, develops rapidly. It is checked only by territorial considerations, or by impact with other developed forms growing from other centres and meeting on a common boundary. Smaller units will be absorbed. As the organisation of agriculture grows more complex, so the social relations arising from it become more elaborate and more pyramidal. Whole new classes may arise—priests, warriors, clerks, local lords and chiefs, all apparently depending on the god-king at the apex. The stabilising element of the whole is the right of the ruler, expressed as religion, as the projection on to him of all those 'loose' affects, all those symbolised social forces, which stand to the individual man as external, heroic realisations of his own limited desires and powers, something holy and apart.

Thus the tutelary deity or chief god of such an economy is closely identified with the god-king, and represents the power of the tribe, city, or kingdom as an associated group of individuals—represents everything in the association which is more than the mere sum of the powers of separate individuals. In so far as the economic production of the society will turn upon sun, wind, rain, and sea he will also invest himself with the affects which man has projected into these natural phenomena. These phenomena have become for him, as they have not for the animal, objects of interest, because their behaviour affects his sowing and reaping and building. Such a society tends to be monotheistic in that the god which expresses the solidarity of the tribe is exalted against all other gods—as Jehovah against Baal—and is held to account for all the successes of this tribe against others. Such a monotheism may become the medium of a whole national resurgence, as when the Semitic tribes of Arabia, a pastoral people, hurled themselves upon the settled peoples of Europe, to the cry, 'We are all one people: join our economy or die.' (There is no God but Allah. Acknowledge him, or pay tribute, or be put to the sword.') It does not exclude however the accompaniment of the tribal god by a host of lesser spirits, cherubim, seraphim, Beelzebub, and other personifications of the forces of nature, as against personifications of the social unity. Yet man's homage to these forces is always more individualistic and personal. The one compelling homage which to ignore is to be really wicked, is the homage to the tribal god.

This pure monotheism cannot exist in a successful agricultural society. It can exist, as the example of Islam shows, in a successful pastoral society, where there is little division of labour and all men are equal beneath the chief—Mohammed, Prophet of God, and his Caliph. Such an equality cannot exist in a society where the pyramiding of function involved in a settled agricultural society has been carried far. There are gradations of sacredness, and the ruling class is hierarchical. For that very reason Mohammedanism comes as a message of hope to an exploited class, and this accounts for its early fierce disruptive power. This necessarily collapsed as soon as a pastoral society, by its conquests and tribute drawing, became transformed into just another Asiatic despotism, and in spite of the survival of the rigid Mohammedan formula with its monotheistic proclamation of pastoral equality, the Mohammedan religion became for the exploited class filled with godlings, beatified disciples, and angels. The religion, though degenerate, is changed by its previous history. Mohammedanism, even in process of becoming another oriental despotism, retains a pastoral flavour of equality. It is more stable, and at a higher plane than the older religions. This in turn reacts upon its economy, which always remains more virile, seafaring, merchandising and nomad than a settled agricultural civilisation.

The pure flame of monotheism may of course be kept alive in an unsuccessful tribe which is not completely extinguished. Thus the Jews, situated on the main trade route of early civilisation and harried and battered on all sides, were compressed into a proud, prickly, bigoted society whose difficult economic life is reflected in their religion. But this very battering toughened them; and made of Judaism a consciousness which, as events proved, was to possess great survival value in the maelstorm of social relations of the East.

Monotheism of this kind is incompatible with despotic Imperialism. When for a brief time the Jewish tribe became

Imperialising, and Solomon was even able to aspire to the hand of Pharaoh's daughter, Solomon took to himself strange gods. The quick collapse of Solomon's empire brought about a return to monotheism and the collapse itself was attributed to the unauthorised additions of Solomon.

When an agricultural kingdom imperialises, the unit it swallows up becomes part of the economy of the kingdom. None the less it retains much of its original structure. For example a Mesopotamian or Nilotic 'city-farm' swallowed up by a monarchy will retain its local governor, who now becomes subordinate to the monarchy; and the local deity who symbolises the forces of the community will pass into the national pantheon. It will depend on the importance of the unit swallowed whether the god or goddess will become incarnate in the tutelary deity of the nation, or merely get a seat in the pantheon, and whether it remains a god or becomes a 'hero.' In any event the local deity will continue to be a cult at the headquarters of the unit. Such imperialism should not be confused with the modern Imperialism or Mohammedan Imperialism, in which two *different* economies one temporarily superior to the other, happen to collide. There is then no fusion of religions for the economies do not fuse. Either the relation is merely one of tribute drawing, in which case the conquered society keeps its economy and religion as in most of India to-day; or else one economy swallows up the other, which therefore adopts (with minor differences) the religion of the conquering race. This is seen in that part of India affected by bourgeois culture, which therefore becomes Westernised and bourgeoisified. It would be better to call the Imperialism of Egypt and China, which resulted in the fusion of the societies involved, 'expansion', rather than Imperialism in the tribute-drawing or bourgeois sense.

Thus a fully developed pantheon, such as that of Egypt, Babylon, China, or India, represents a kind of telescoping of the social history of the peoples involved. The various incarnations of the ruling deity, and the other occupants of the pantheon, represent swallowed social units (such as the nomes of Egypt) of greater or less importance. Myths, such as that of Isis and Osiris or the Chinese Sky-goddess, embody a magic account of the society's economic production. Other natural forces enter as 'promoted' spirits or ghosts, and the development of warrior and learned classes, and of all other forms of division of labour, results in gods presiding over such activities. The tutelary god has a prime Minister or Vizier, a secretary, a wife. The profane family is reflected in a holy one. The inverted world of religion acquires a bewildering complexity, has a long history of its own, and exerts a reciprocal effect on the society which engenders it. The labours of archaeologists on the records of Egypt, Babylon, China, India, Assyria, Persia, and Crete can only partially uncover this history, for the most living part of religion, its ritual and its active social being, is lost. Only the bones of the organism remain. None the less enough remains to make increasingly clear the accuracy of Marx's analysis, based on the work of Morgan and Feuerbach.

Communities which exist by gardening, instead of agriculture, and where such gardening is (as still to-day in Africa) the monopoly of women, will worship a Mighty Mother, symbolising in female form the productive forces of the tribe. Since the males of such tribes are generally war-like, the Mighty Mother will be accompanied by a war-god, standing to her in the equivocal relation of husband and son.

Because a division of labour continually secures increased productivity, a civilisation of this character—the settled agricultural culture of Egypt, Persia, China, Mexico, Peru, India, and Mesopotamia—continues to fuse into increasingly centralised despotisms. The individual in whose person all the forces of such a society are concentrated, the god-king, therefore becomes increasingly awful and sacred. Those individuals who regard all the forces wielded by society as alien to them become increasingly humble, for the discrepancy between their individual powers and the power wielded by society in the person of the despot has become enormous. Caught up in the elaboration of the economic process, they are mere passive labouring units—slaves.

This religious alienation of themselves from the forces of society, this religious 'humility', is of course the reflex of a similar alienation in the realm of right or law. The products of society seem to an increasing extent to be due, not to them as individuals but to the forces arising from their association, which forces as we have seen, are all concentrated in the person of the god-king. The god-king comes therefore to own all these products, and to his subjects is granted only as much as will maintain them alive, and even this is a gift of the God-king, springing from his beneficence and mercy, and in no way a right due to them from him.

Meanwhile, round the god-king cluster all the administrative, clerical, priestly and warrior castes who receive a portion of the sacred effulgence of the monarch, for they too are custodians of part of the forces of society, and therefore with a qualified right in its products. Unlike the lower class—the subjects, slaves, or common people—this class has rights and privileges, and a sacredness which, while less than the despots, is still enough to separate them from the rightless. In a highly developed agricultural economy, there are products over and to spare beyond what is needed to maintain alive the exploited class.

This official class or aristocracy is naturally interested in the maintenance of the system, yet their own sacredness and the fact that the running of all the forces of society is in their hands, give them a less absolute belief in the official religion. They have a strong sceptical tendency, and invariably generate a 'refined' religion of their own, free from the 'superstitions' of the 'mob', such as the Confucianism of China, the 'esoteric' teaching of Egypt, and the Brahmanic 'philosophy' of India. Hence, should the god-king prove personally obnoxious, they have little hesitation in replacing him by a palace-revolution.

There can be only one end to such a class society. There is an increasing split between the ruling class and the active, exploited class. The one becomes more and more functionless, parasitic, and 'philosophic', and the other more and more exploited, miserable, and superstitious. The productive process falls more and more into the hands of the 'ignorant class', who are pressed still more keenly for tribute, until a general impoverishment of agriculture and failure of the national economy begins to take place.

Such a culture soon becomes a hollow shell, which still keeps up a semblance of vigour, but is in fact slowly decaying. Its decay may last several centuries. The revolt of the exploited class will be sporadic and disorganised, for the nature of an economy of this kind is not such as to develop in the toilers the qualities which will make them in their turn able to rule. Such a decaying culture may split up into a number of feudal units, and revitalise itself because, in so doing, each local chief rallies round him as supporters his local exploited clan, and to do so improves their lot. The process will however only be repeated again, and out of local provinces will rise another Emperor. Or the kingdom may be exploited by a similar kingdom at a more vigorous stage of development. Or it may be over-run by pastoral invaders who with their more equalitarian social relations will revitalise the economy, only to see the kingdom perish once again in the misery of the exploited class as the economy drops.

This is the history of what Marx called the 'Asiatic' form of culture. It explains the despotisms, decays, disruptions, and dragging deaths-in-life of the great Empires of Egypt, Mesopotamia, India, China, and Central and South America. All such empires are based on a settled agricultural economy involving irrigation works and the extensive co-ordination of agriculture. Their religion reflects this development and the way in which man's self-feeling which has lost itself is projected in an inverted world. Inverted—because man's abject humiliation before the forces of that world is a parody of his own exaltation by association in society. Yet as a parody, it is also criticism. Because of his humility, his exaltation is alienated from him and invested in another. The powers he creates are assumed by the ruling class, before which he abases himself. The law of his society, which includes his self-alienation from the goods he produces, is just that distortion of the real facts of social life which generates the inverted world of religion. Thus we see what Marx meant when he said that religion is an inverted consciousness of the world because that world is itself an inverted world. The exploited class, which is the real source of the productive power of society, places itself at the bottom of the pyramid by giving to the parasitic class the whole of the goods it produces beyond the bare minimum necessary for existence. The overt social structure is itself an inversion of the reality behind it. At first the ruling class is functional: as it becomes more sacred and division of labour grows it becomes more functionless and parasitic. Such a world becoming constantly more fully inverted is just the world which produces a more and more elaborate religion acting as a counterbalance. Finally, from having been a vital factor in economic production, magic, grown into developed religion, has become the bulwark of a functionless class and therefore one of the fetters on economic production.

* * * *

Into such an inverted world are necessarily projected all the distortions caused by the discrepancy between society's outward forms and its real content. Such a society feeds its exploited with products belonging 'of right' entirely to the rulers: therefore the divinities are kind and generous. The feeding, the very life of the exploited class depends entirely on a society in which they are alienated from the means of production: therefore their whole existence and life is dependent on God, and since all good things, all force and power and knowledge, are resident in society, the misery can only come from another source, either from an anti-god or devil, or from their selves—from their sinfulness. Thus sin, which in primitive society is restricted to anti-social acts—the breaking of taboos or the malconduct of magical ceremonies—becomes in more developed societies an almost permanent condition of the populace. The religious dream life, by a well-known mechanism, becomes a compensation or reflex of the waking life. In proportion as life becomes more miserable and deprived, one's dreams become richer and more full of content. In dreams, man's ghost seems to wander and leave the body, and thus it becomes an article of such religions that in a future life the ghost, wandering in the other, inverted world, will inherit all the good things of that world.

Separate, ghostly existence as a concept is a result of dream. Immortal or long enduring existence as a concept is the result of the transmission by society of history and names and it is true that in this traditional other-world of society's, men's emanations do enjoy a life beyond life. This abstract fact becomes fantastically concrete in religion. At first this life beyond life is a perquisite of the king or famous men and so more accurately reflects the social basis of the belief; but as the economy develops and an exploited class grows, its urgent misery drives it to a demand for other-worldly goods. Since these ghostly goods can be granted without depriving the ruling class of real goods, the common people finds itself—for what it is worth—in possession of the fantastic privileges of its betters, to lead a life beyond life in the inverted world of religion. Successive layers of excavation clearly reveal this process in Egypt, where the immortality associated with funerary rites, at first a perquisite of the god-king, gradually filters down to all classes. This fantastic realisation which is at once the expression of real *misery* and a protest against that *real* misery, which is the sigh of the hard-pressed creature, therefore, like a neurotic or psychotic compensatory mechanism, acts as a stabilising factor against the growing misery of the people. Religion now finally, in the course of this long development, has become a safety-valve—the opium of the people. In the last stages such a society's religion has as its most important content, not a pantheon of power, but salvation, release from sin (i.e. from temporal misery), eternal life, divine love and consolation and fatherhood—or motherhood. It has become the 'soul' of a soulless world.

*   *   *   *

But even the god-king's will is subject to checks. His prayers for harvest do not always prevail: this cannot be always interpreted as the sin of his people. Floods and earthquakes and pestilences come. Man, in spite of economic production, has not completely subdued nature. In other words the gods who symbolise the powers of economic production, are not all-powerful. There is a process which even they cannot subdue.

This process therefore emerges as Fate, Law, Kismet, Karma, as a mechanical set process which even gods must obey. Because man is still projecting his self-feeling into nature, this force appears as a Will, but because it is distinguished from the gods it is a disembodied Will or something woven mechanically from a thread. This Will is the residue of magic. It represents magic's recognition—after it has reached the more thoughtful and stabilised interpenetration with reality involved in an economic production that is religious—that there are things beyond the power of economic production. This disembodied Will, which sucks within itself all those phenomena proved not amenable to economic production but observed as a result of economic production, is therefore both the negation and the product of magic. It is the recognition, first of an arbitrary will, later (as we shall see) of a Law which even the gods—i.e., society—cannot override. It is causality or determination in embryo. As society develops, determinism develops, for all society's explorations of reality as a result of economic production, generate fresh evidence of processes which cannot be overridden. But just because they cannot be overridden, they can be predicted. They can be *used*. Causality or Kismet, becoming science, is once again fused with the economic production it at first negated. Society, by becoming conscious of necessity, becomes free of it.

Asiatic culture cannot, however, reach such a full understanding. The most refined philosophies of the ruling class of such a culture (Chinese and Indian) can only see reality as a theatre of wills or projected affects, for the overt forms of their societies depend on various rights to effect one's will, to dispose arbitrarily according to one's individual desire of one's land and subjects. The real content of the society is veiled from them, for such a world is an inverted world. The power of such a society does not in fact inhere in their wills but in the actions of the ruled class. Creativity does not flow from their desires as such, but only in so far as their desires enter as an active component into the actions of the exploited class and so into the productive movement of society.

In so far as their wills are *opposed* to the productive movement of society, they are merely obstructive, sucked of their real content, illusory and fantastic. To understand this would be to cease to be a ruling class, *owning* the means of production, and to become specialists, *working* the means of production. Hence such societies cannot advance beyond a philosophy of idealism, in which Will and Mind are dominant and Ideas have a supra-material, absolute existence outside the heads of men. Such an idealism is tawdry and limited because it commits the thinker to a closed, eternal world bound inside the categories of present theory, instead of presenting an open, timeful world in which theory is growing and enriching itself in active penetration of matter. In the same way this society's idea of causality, symbolised as Fate, can never escape from an arbitrariness, an air of magic and subjectivity, because cause is always seen as cause by a conscious force, or entity, which is simply the ruling class's affective will projected into reality as an absolute.

In India, with its streams of invaders and constant movement, such a culture produces the pullulating pantheon of Hinduism, or achieves, in the Empire of Asoka, the metaphysical nihilism of Buddhism, in which society, having achieved its utmost limit, cannot escape from its social fetters or the infection of an exploited class, and sees stretching before it in all its helplessness, the iron wheel of things, from which it would be a blessing to escape. Man seems to find himself for a moment in Buddhism, only to lose himself, for it is the product of a ruling class grown pessimistic of its office, and seeing blessedness as the cessation of will. It survives only by becoming a new religion, full of 'salvation' and divine love. In China, more shielded from invasion, the same development produces a static, rigid pantheon in the sky, with the causality of the Way above it, and at its apex the divine son of the Sky-Goddess, the Emperor, incarnation of the social forces on earth.

China and South and Central America remained units in isolation. India became a melting pot of invading waves. But Egypt, and to a lesser degree Babylonia and Crete, as centres of a more stable civilisation gradually exported to the fringes of the Mediterranean their wheat and settled agricultural production—all the technique which had made them elaborate centres of despotism. In the differing physical conditions of Greece, Asia Minor and Italy, however, this technique never advanced beyond the formation of city states. By the time these states had developed to the stage of small kingdoms, based on cities, settled agricultural production had ceased to be the main productive force of the societies they represented. They became, by reason of their topographical situation and the natural development of their fishing activities, real trading centres. Their smallness as units, separated by mountains and straits, encouraged trade—the sea was handy and a general highway. Shipbuilding and the like they already had from Egypt. Thus a new society emerged, in which the productive forces of society were disguised and made complex by the intervention of trafficking, and there was a numerous class which did not owe its position or its power to its specific place in the agricultural division of labour, but seemed to snatch its wealth out of the air. Such a society was even further confused by the incursion of pastoral peoples, as conquering waves, who imposed for a short time an alien economy, pantheon and social organisation upon the peoples they subdued.

Thus an entirely new economic development took place in which the city, as the trading centre, acquired a hegemony over agriculture, and the ruling class was at least partly a trading class. Such states, with their competitive basis, are necessarily disruptive—they are 'free' states quarrelling always about their privileges and freedoms, jealous of the liberties of their markets, and only reluctantly combining in the face of a common danger. It was bourgeoisdom in embryo, but the basis of all such states still remained agricultural, and the slave class created by settled agricultural economy was taken over, as a system, by the 'free' pastoral peoples and became the basic relation of agriculture and commodity production generally. Hence, in spite of the market for commodities, there was no market for labour-power—only for slaves. The conditions were not yet ripe for the development of bourgeois economy.

In such societies the tutelary deity of the city symbolised the productive forces of society, and production revolved round the city with its protective walls, and the domain it ruled. The god-king or hero or mighty mother of the local economy appears to fuse with the local pantheon of the incoming pastoral people—the father patriarch and his family. The more equalitarian economy of the pastoral people results in the gathering round the petty, divine king of a gerontocracy who ultimately depose him and are themselves—in Athens and elsewhere—deposed by the rising merchant class who form a democracy. This marks the apex of Greek development, and in Rome takes the form of the transfer from the senatorial to the 'knightly' class. The very strife between the agricultural and merchant ruling classes is insoluble within the framework of a slave-owning society, and ultimately brings about the break-down of Hellenic economy. But before its collapse it has given birth, in the momentary efflorescence of Athenian, Ionian and Corinthian prosperity, to the culture whose bold speculation reflects the scepticism and untraditional cosmopolitanism of the rising merchant classes. Hellenic philosophy, however, in spite of its moments of splendid balance, never escapes from the limitations of a slave-owning class whose slaves, interposed as a buffer between themselves and nature, prevent their philosophy emerging as completely positive and scientific. In Ionia it is revolutionary: with Plato more conservative: always it is fresh and critical, but always it is unable to get beyond a self-feeling which has not found itself. It remains a religious philosophy, which projects Will into nature, sees causality as Fate or Divine Law, and explains reality in terms of human Purposes, Forms or Ideas existing independently of human brains or real matter.

In its prime able to overturn the despotism of the East and penetrate into India, Greece becomes, as slave-owning develops on a merchant basis, the centre of intolerable antagonisms. It thus falls a victim to the centralised despotic monarchy. The Empires with their god-kings come into being again. Merchant towns, such as Alexandria, remain the centre of scepticism and a critical attitude to divinity, but the demoralisation of the slaves is reflected in the universal reign of the various mystery religions, full of salvation and immortal life. They had existed in the early agricultural despotisms of Mycenean civilisation (Demeter and the Eleusinian mysteries) but had sunk into the background with the invasion of the Hellenes. These Hellenes had a full-blooded pastoral economy, in which life, lived to the full in this world, required only a short, shadow existence in the next. The mystery religions emerged triumphantly again when this Hellenic rejuvenation, so brief and glorious, in turn produced an enormous exploited class, demanding in its inverted world the life denied it in the real world.

While therefore the East continued its old despotisms, and the Greek god-kings flourished, blown upon by scepticism only in the cities, Rome was establishing in Italy a hegemony which no Greek city, with its less favourable topography, was able to achieve. Rome too had an agricultural god-king (Saturn) who was replaced by a pastoral god-patriarch (Jove). In Rome too, therefore, it may be supposed that a pastoral people conquered a settled agricultural people, and the resulting fusion begot a king and a gerontocracy (the senate) which finally deposed the king, and was itself deposed by a trading class. It is no accident that Rome on the Tiber was a trading centre, and the emergence of her senate and equestrian classes must have been due to the emergence of a merchant class beneath the veil of agricultural and pastoral social relations. This class rapidly becomes a predatory and powerful class, its army of 'citizens' being far superior to Oriental despotisms or more decadent Greek cities. Its religion, so similar to the Greek, yet reflects the greater insularity and 'purity' of Roman development, farther removed from Egyptian and Eastern ideology. Patriarchial relations, relics of a pastoral people, affect the ideology of the ruling class and give it a sternness and absoluteness in its dealings with other peoples that is regarded as typically Roman.

The spread of Roman influence necessarily involves the creation of a huge predatory class, the senatorial and knightly, whose increasing wealth is the reflection of the increasing exploitation, unknown to those Asiatic despotisms in which the ruling class at least remains part and parcel of the economy it exploits. The Roman ruling class is, however, a trading, absentee class. Such a non-functional class, in which the forces of society seem to be wielded by men who take no active interest in the worlds they rule, gives rise to stoicism, in which the gods are absentee landlords, and the world shuffles on as well as it can. Such a religion can only arise in a general demoralisation such as that which overtook the Roman world in the last years of the Republic. The absentee, predatory class, by their very absenteeism, had prepared their own downfall, and it was possible first for Caesar and then Augustus and his successors to rule through an administrative class of freemen, a new bureaucracy whose creation involves the death of the older exploiters. The Roman Empire takes on more and more Oriental characteristics, and, as slave-owning economy develops again on the basis of local and centralised bureaucracies, with the trading cities included in the social plexus, we have the final stage of classical economy. The pivot of the stage has become the god-king, the Emperor, who rules his people as the master rules his slaves, and in whom seem concentrated all the productive forces of society. Beneath him are grouped an aristocracy who derive their 'sacredness' from him and regard him with veiled scepticism. Their own religion is some or other form of a refined idealistic philosophy, which in a certain gap opened between the gods and reality, reflects the complexity of this stage of economy, in which the god-king rules indirectly through various channels and no longer dwells in the midst of society as in the simpler Egyptian despotism. But to the vast exploited class the god-king and the tutelary deity he represents, is still the incarnation of the forces of society. Round him clusters whatever cult or pantheon has been inherited, but his figure is central and he guarantees the Roman Law, creation of the new bureaucracy, which secures the smooth functioning of the productive economy, and at once oppresses them and keeps them this side of extinction.

* * * *

Such a society can only repeat the history of past despotisms. The cleavage between the slave-owners and the slaves, the vain rebellion of the slaves, brings about an increasing exploitation of the slave and serf classes, and an increasing impoverishment of society. The structure, because of its complexity, size, and military efficiency, is not as yet challengeable by any other power outside.

It is however challenged by an internal power. Christianity appears, a new religion in which the eternal happiness promised by mystery religions in the next world is to be realised in this world by the practice of a new form of social relations—primitive communism. Each church is a group of the faithful holding all material goods in common, in possession of salvation, and waiting until Christ their King shall return to earth and realise the millenium in the universal reign of primitive communism. Whatever gave this programme its detailed form, however much it owed to the Essenes, to the Galilean village economy, to the personality of Christ, and to the nationalism of Palestine, it was evidently the bodying forth of the aspirations of the exploited class. It is a religion of revolution.

It is misleading to regard Christianity as simply another 'mystery' religion (such as Mithraism or the cult of Isis) which because of some superior attractiveness carried the day against its rivals. This is to see religion not as a social reality but as the adventure of an idea. The Isis and Mithraistic cults were ordinary products of Asiatic misery and classical decay, promising in the next world salvation and healing for the miseries of this. Christianity was distinct from religions of this kind because of its tougher, this-worldly content. The millenium was to come in this world, the Kingdom of Heaven was to be realised *here*. It was led by a revolutionary figure—Christ, whose apparently unsuccessful rebellion had according to his disciples really been a triumph.

For a long time now the Roman Empire had been decaying, so that the social relations it represented had become a fetter on the productive powers. The god-Emperor and his staff had ceased to be functional units of society and had become mere tax-gathering and defence organs which were not even working efficiently as such. The decay of communications and the loosening of the economic cords that had held the Empire together, drove the god-king and his staff wildly about the Empire in an attempt to hold together with the superstructure of law and administration what was already falling apart as the result of the increasing decomposition of agriculture. The Empire was returning whence it had sprung, as the result of the impoverishment of the soil by latifundia and the general demoralisation of the exploited class. Local landlords were leaving their estates wholesale because of the increasing relative burden of taxation.

This economic devolution was reflected in the growth of Christianity, particularly in the large towns which as the bonds slackened were naturally the first to feel the functionlessness of the god-Emperor's *régime*. Christianity was the equivalent of a nationalist movement, but no nations existed in the cosmopolitan Roman Empire. The choice was between the city or local community and the Empire. The nearest to a nationalist movement was in Jerusalem and it was precisely in Jerusalem that Christianity arose round the person of a typical Jewish prophet, Jesus. The local exploiting class of Jerusalem, the 'Scribes and Pharisees,' had however come to terms with the conqueror, the relation somewhat resembling that between the British Government and the de Valera Government in Ireland. Although their interests are opposed, both are rooted in the same class society and both therefore are opposed to a Workers' Republic of the type now being fought for there.* Jesus evidently also had in mind a 'People's Republic,' in which goods would be shared in common, there would be neither master nor man, and exploitation would cease. He believed it however to be possible within the framework of the existing State ('Render unto Caesar the things that are Caesar's'). In other words, he did not regard it as necessary that the seizure of power should take place as a preliminary to the inauguration of the People's Commune or Kingdom of Heaven on Earth, the idea of which—so poetically and idealistically unfolded—secured him his tremendous support among the working class of Palestine who listened to his denunciations of the rich.

This reformist instead of revolutionary approach was just what secured the defeat of Christianity. Such demonstrations as that of the entry into Jerusalem showed the wide measure of popular support he had obtained, but with no programme of action directed to the seizure of power, this basis of popular support was useless. Jesus appears to have hesitated a long time before the choice of appearing as the Messiah and so focusing the nationalistic aspirations of the Jews. He finally claimed the position, yet as a Messiah who would not seize power but assume it by prayer, by 'magic.' Such was not the Jewish conception of the Messiah; it seemed indeed to sincere Jewish patriots a betrayal of the national revolution, and a familiar situation was enacted when the Pharisees consolidated their power and that of the Roman bosses on whom they depended by an impudent appeal to the national feeling of the Jews. Jesus was thus branded as a blasphemer—as 'anti-social.'

* Circa 1936. (Ed.)

Thus, by his treatment of the vital question of workers' power, Jesus had from the start ensured the defeat of his communist programme. That part of the programme which involved the actual coming into being of the communist state became inverted, because it was to come into being in a reformist way by its own ideal appeal—miraculously. The Kingdom of Heaven therefore gradually became 'the millenium' and eventually was altogether shifted into another world. The misery of the exploited classes of the Roman Empire was first reflected as a revolutionary possibility now, but finally became a dream, a compensatory wish-fulfilment like that of other mystery religions, a fantastic salvation criticising and yet stabilising real misery here. This reformist step appears to have been taken by Christ at the very moment when he forbade Peter to use violence. He was prepared to whip the money-changers out of the Temple but not out of the State. This fact itself reflected the inability of the exploited classes of the Roman Empire to organise a revolt with any success. In spite of Christ's denunciation of rich men, a policy of class collaboration was forced on Christianity by the demoralisation of the workers.

When Jesus was executed, therefore, it was natural that instead of regarding this as the first defeat in a long revolutionary war certain of ultimate victory (as the proletariat regarded the defeat of the Paris Commune) the followers of Jesus decided to see it as an other-worldly triumph, as a wish-fulfilment victory. But this apparently astute move—no doubt quite naïve and sincere—while it appeared to consolidate Christianity, also finally consolidated the reformist element in it. Since Jesus's victory was already realised, it was merely a matter of waiting for the Kingdom to come into being. The emphasis had already shifted from revolution in this world to salvation in the next. None the less the tougher quality of Christianity as compared to the mystery religions was shown in the fact that at least the Kingdom of Heaven was to be realised soon *in this world.* The end of the world (i.e., the beginning of the ideal world-commune) was *at hand.*

The propagandist element of Christianity now centred in the organisation of the Churches and the love-feast. This was an attempt (rather like the modern co-operative movement) to realise the primitive communism of the Kingdom of Heaven within the framework of the existing state, through autonomous local communities.

All goods were to be held in common and administered by officials, the poor were to be cared for. All were equal within the Church or commune. The organisation had therefore something of the character, not only of a co-operative movement but of early forms of trade union organisation with their friendly and benefit activities. Such centres could be made active organs of revolutionary activity in the Roman Empire.

The movement grew rapidly. It had of course the advantage of dissemination in the first stages by a cosmopolitan body, the Jews, who were most active and influential in precisely those places—the large towns—where devolutionary tendencies were most strongly marked. The fact that Jesus had been executed by the native exploiting class prevented Christianity from being a Jewish national movement, and it soon spread to the uncircumcised.

It became dangerous to the Empire when it began to attract to itself all those elements of the ruling classes in the towns and in the army who found themselves in opposition to the centralising government of the Empire. These were the landlords so heavily taxed that they had to be ordered to remain on their estates, and the dispossessed and expropriated aristrocrats and knights. These, corresponding to the declassed or revolutionary *petite bourgeoisie* of to-day, gave a stiffening to what had been mainly a slave or *lumpen proletarian* movement. Thus stiffened and organised, Christianity had the courage openly to challenge the existing State power. Christians refused to worship the god-Emperor. Since the god-Emperor was the embodiment and focus of the social forces of the Empire this was an open revolutionary act ; and it was accompanied by the formation of illegal self-governing units, the Church communes, which were just as revolutionary challenges to the existing fabric of social relations as the denial of the Emperor's divinity.

In spite of the general looseness and decay of the Roman Empire this challenge had to be met, and whenever an efficient Emperor was functioning, it was met by a vigorous counter-revolutionary drive. All the familiar apparatus of counter-revolution—slander, espionage, whipping up of racial feeling (the 'Nazarenes') and provocative acts (Nero's burning of Rome)—were used in the struggle. Of course the general dissolution of the Roman Empire ensured that for long periods and in many provinces no counter-revolutionary movement at all took place.

Christianity survived the persecution well. The growing burden of centralism produced a communist and devolutionary feeling everywhere. The Army and the Civil Service were infected with it ; it even invaded the Emperor's household. But Christianity had been committed by Jesus to a fatal policy, that of passive resistance, or non-co-operation. It is therefore possible that in the collapsing Roman Empire Christianity played the same role as Gandhism in the collapsing British Empire in India and was the means whereby revolt was canalised and turned into safe forms of activity.

This itself in India is a reflection of the fact that Gandhism is a peasant movement and the peasants form a class which is not a class, which owing to the peasant's isolation cannot act in an organised manner; its members can act only as individuals. An individual cannot revolt forcibly; he cannot set himself up against the whole State. He can only resist passively 'to the death.' This Christ did, and so did all the revolutionary elements among his followers. The less revolutionary elements recanted until the storms blew over and this of course strengthened ultimately the forces of reformism in the Church. The Roman exploited class was a slave class divided into households and latifundia and therefore unorganised. Christianity was an attempt to achieve such an organisation on a metropolitan and area basis, or, in the legions (where Christian cells were formed) on a functional basis. But the whole pressure of rebellion was towards decentralisation, and it was perhaps inevitable that Christian revolt should be passive and non-co-operative. Certainly it was correct in not attempting to bolster up or seize the Imperial power, for it was this power which was obsolete. Christianity's rôle was to strengthen the decentralising movements within the Empire by setting up autonomous local communes tied by fraternal understanding. These were the Churches. But the early Christians were not prepared to fight for the existence of these communes, and it was this which brought about the defeat of the whole revolutionary movement.

The most efficient Roman Emperor, Diocletian, attempted to combat revolution with reform. While launching a vigorous counter-revolution or 'persecution', he also introduced a considerable amount of decentralisation in the Empire, dividing it into four autonomous units. Although this move was probably inevitable, it merely hastened the disintegration of the Empire. Its increasing impoverishment was bringing about a rapid devolution.

In remote Britain, however, Constantine had seen the creative rôle of Christianity and its absolute inevitability in the advanced disintegration of the Empire. Local autonomy was bound to come. With great shrewdness, he saw that Christianity had also advanced to a stage where it could be relied upon to co-operate with the powers against which it was originally in revolt. Himself of proletarian origin, Constantine understood precisely the rôle Christianity was playing in relation to the masses. Like Hitler in a Germany 'menaced' with Socialism, Constantine, faced with the menace of Christianity saw how to make this revolutionary feeling the means of bringing him to power, not as a revolutionary leader but within the framework of the existing State. Thus Constantine's legions, like Hitler's Nazis, having been promised the full programme of revolution, swept him to power, after which he found no difficulty in consolidating his position within the Imperial machine and dropping the revolutionary programme.

In order to understand his success, it is necessary to bear in mind the part played by the leaders of social democracy in the period 1890--1936. They found themselves, like the Christian bishops, priests and deacons, as elected officials of organisations which were revolutionary in aim, having as their goal in one case the establishment of socialism and in the other, the establishment of the Kingdom of Heaven (primitive communism), but both designed to realise part of their revolutionary aims *now*—the trades unions and parliamentary parties by gaining wage concessions within the framework of capitalism, the Churches by friendly and benefit activities among the poor. The elected officials soon became permanent ones and eventually they found themselves with commanding positions, honours, and vested interests in maintaining on the one hand the existing society and on the other hand the revolutionary organisation which gave them their job. Hence the social democratic leaders in all countries played the same part. They were prepared to co-operate in all vital matters with the ruling class—the maintenance of law and order, the waging of Imperialist war, the sabotaging of political strikes or demonstrations, the stifling of extra-parliamentary action, and the crushing of revolutionary socialism (Bolshevism). At the same time they kept their organisations alive by the expression of revolutionary sentiments, and by attacking the ruling class on minor issues.

Constantine evidently found that the development of Christianity had produced in the revolutionary movement just such a class of leaders. They were willing to 'go over' to the god-king in return for being given an important place in the administration of the Empire. The administrative class as a whole had no hesitation, in view of the general scepticism of such an epoch, in 'embracing' Christianity. The Church became Imperial and the bulwark of the god-king's power. The completely insincere nature of Constantine's bargain with Christianity is shown by the fact that he himself never became a Christian.

Thus the forces of the Christian revolutionary movement were placed at the service of the counter-revolution. The priests became State officials and the Churches State organs. All the revolutionary content of the Christian programme, the Kingdom of Heaven, the millenium, was shifted entirely into the next world. The love-feast, at which material food was shared in common, became the ideal sacrifice of the Mass in which only a 'token' food was shared out. The communion of goods dwindled to the administration of a poor law by the priests. Christianity became a mystery-religion, full of the neo-Platonism, Mithraism and Isis-cult remnants derived from earlier mystery religions. At the very moment when it buttressed the greed of the upper classes, it started to preach to the lower the virtues of abstinence, fasting, poverty, and self-denial. Such a betrayal was of course only possible with a movement which had already been bewildered, and from the start, by the reformism of Jesus's fatal choice:—'Render unto Caesar the things that are Caesar's and to God the things that are God's,' which seemed at the time such a clever escape from a difficult political situation. This bewilderment was made permanent by the hailing of Jesus's execution as an other-worldly triumph, not a this-worldly set-back. This again had seemed a clever move at the time. Yet, like Socialism in Germany and Italy, Christianity had been defeated by this refusal to place in the forefront the vital question of power.

Of course the step taken by Constantine had been prepared by the development of Roman economy. The leaders of Christianity had already become wealthy and influential persons in the society of their time. Constantine's action therefore only regularised a process which had long been going on below the surface. By incorporating Christianity into the superstructure he stiffened it and enabled the Roman Empire to survive, at least in the East. Christianity itself was of course transformed in the process and became Greek Orthodoxy, an organ of the State with a ritual, a pantheon, and a Hellenistic monotheism which reflected the despotic Imperialism round which it was built.

* * * *

The impoverishment of the Roman Empire, increasing the incidence of taxation, had expropriated large numbers of the land-owning class, in spite of the edicts forbidding them to give up their estates. The attempt by the central authority to squeeze still more surplus value from their slaves often resulted in the nominal 'freeing' of slaves, and the creation of serfs. It was in these circumstances that the local landowners, as well as the slaves, had welcomed the freedom from centralised responsibility involved in the communism of primitive Christianity. In the finish Roman Imperial economy became an economy of local peasants, serfs, decaying cities and harassed landowners. The revolutionary content of Christianity now appeared as the revolt, not (as originally) of the common people, but of the local ruling class. The Arian heresy and its successors was one form of this: the breaking away of the Western Church was another.

Meanwhile the barbarians penetrated the Empire—partly by importation, to swell the declining population of the Empire, partly by actual conquest. They were sucked in rather than invading it. Their social relations and pastoral conceptions of status were more suited to an economy in which wealth and money were vanishing.

In this disintegration the Church in the West acted as a bulwark of the older civilisation only because she was a bulwark of the older economy. In the worst days of the Roman Empire, when reduction in population became a social virtue, communities of men and women vowed to chastity had assembled in the attempt to form a new communism, now that it was no longer faced by a centralised and powerful government, proved successful, and everywhere the Benedictine monastry sprang up, and became the manor—the model agricultural unit. Meanwhile the secular clergy, the bishop and the priest, had become intimately associated with the economic life of the neighbourhood in a way impossible to the Imperial agent. When the barbarians trickled in, the Imperial tax-gathering bureaucracy fled, but the priests and bishops, drawing and consuming their tribute locally, stayed on. Thus the invaders found themselves confronted by a homogeneity of organisation in the regions they penetrated, which was intimately associated with the very life of the land. To disrupt this would be to disrupt life itself, for economic production would cease. At the same time the disappearance of the Imperial agents, the number of absentee local landowners, and the decentralising tendency of the Western Church, made it possible for the land to be parcelled between barbarians and Church without disaster. Thus Christendom stood for these barbarians as something universal and ordered and civilised—a Law given in the nature of things—for the whole superior economy they penetrated and took over revolved round it. They were therefore 'converted', and not only were they themselves changed but they also changed Christianity and increased the decentralising trend of the Church by giving Christianity a 'barbarian' form. Feudal social relations thus came into being and, just as barbarians adopted the church, the church adopted feudal forms of land tenure.

The Western Church found itself faced with the complete break-up of its European organisation as the result of feudal autonomy. The only remedy was celibacy, and this already existed in embryo in the form of monastic chastity, itself a product of the dwindling of the Roman Empire's wealth and the hallmark of a failing agricultural economy. By making its officials celibate, the Church avoided the dynastic trends of other Imperial officials, who had made hereditary what was originally a delegated power. Celibacy preserved the centralised control of the Church without the need for Imperial stratagems such as the continual shifting of officials. A bishop could be safely allowed to become part and parcel of the life of his neighbourhood, without the danger of his founding a dynasty. This celibacy in itself brought about a separation between priestly and secular branches of the ruling class unknown to any previous civilisations. Without it, undoubtedly, the Western Church would have disintegrated and disappeared into a number of local churches.

Thus Christendom emerged in Western Europe as the one universal idea because it was the one universal organisation. Its courts, its law, its universal provision of salvation, justice and learning, and its alms-giving activities, were but the reflection of its standardising and organising role in the economy of Western Europe. There was a coming and going of scholars and merchandise and commodities, there was exchange of learning, a homogeneity of social relations, a standardisation of agriculture and viticulture in Western Europe, precisely because bishop and monastery provided an interweaving substratum of organised agriculture and trade, a higher level of technical production, which prevented the Dark Ages from being really dark, from ever relapsing into the anarchy of unorganised units. The clerical class was the clerkly class, charged with the keeping of accounts, of farm records, and all the administrative duties essential to an organised agriculture. This power in society, transcending local and territorial boundaries, was expressed in the hierarchy of heaven, with its centralised Divine administration, its God, and the god-king on earth—the Pope of Rome, and his various sacred representatives, bishops, priests, and monks. It was expressed in the towns, made possible by the organisation of *Christian* economy, and therefore rightly centred round the cathedral, the brilliant expression of feudal life.

But the 'lay' landlords, with their unfeudalised, dynastic basis, found themselves, as they grew in intelligence and organisation, eventually in sharp conflict with a celibate, centralised, ecclesiastical organisation. The growing feudal concentration expressed itself not only as a steady transformation of social relations, but as a violent antagonism between the feudal lords themselves, between the various summits of the lay feudal pyramids—the monarchies, and between these and the Church, and the growing bourgeois class in the towns; while exploited by them all was the mass of peasants, descendants of the serfs and slaves of Imperial Rome. Feudal landlordism was in any case doomed: ultimately it would succumb to a centralised monarchy which would itself be only a stage in the emergence of the bourgeois class created in the rising medieval towns. In different countries the antagonism took different forms. Where the monarchy and the bourgeois class joined against a weakened feudalism, assisted by the oppressed peasantry, a breach was made in all the fixed privileges of feudalism. A Reformation, the first step in the bourgeois Revolution, then took place.

This Reformation voiced the demands of bourgeois production in the clearest way. Salvation was no longer the monopoly of the feudal state organisation, but of the individual freely electing for it. The Church was not a body of faithful bound by overtly symbolised social relations (prayers for the dead, Purgatory, the Community of the Saints) but a mere collection of individuals who sank or swam separately according to the grace of God.

God now became arbitrary and dreadful. Corresponding to a society where the individual appears to be naked, dependent entirely on his own efforts in the face of nature, and where all social relations such as alms-giving, craft agreements and price regulations were abandoned as fetters on development, Calvinism emerged. In this form of religion God's will seemed immovable by the prayer of society and confronted only the bare individual. Like an outside Fate, it damned or saved him arbitrarily, not in spite of but through his efforts. Thus Protestantism accurately expressed the true character of the bourgeois society in which the individual is most subject to external 'accident', most helpless and unfree in the face of Fate, precisely because it is the society in which nominally the individual is most free and most able to develop his inner will.

Many 'heresies', such as that of the Albigenses, had before this expressed the revolt of the exploited classes against the feudal landlords. Only a revolt led by the bourgeoisie and based on the large towns, could be successful. Bourgeois and peasants and monarch were able for a time to make common cause because their enemies were at that stage the same—the big feudal lords.

Catholicism and Calvinism, one representing the feudal class, the other the bourgeois class, struggle and achieve various compromises: the compromise of the English Church (which is battered first by the Puritan Revolution and then by the Industrial, Methodist and non-conformist, Revolution, both representing developing petty bourgeois interests): the compromise of the Gallican Church (with a greater feudal mixture, which is shattered by the French Revolution); of the various German Churches; of the Spanish Church (in which the Crown ends by being identified again with the feudal, land-owning grandees); and of the Netherlands. In all cases the bourgeois is placed in the same anomalous position, in that the real fulfilment of his creed—complete absence of social restraints—would lead either to anarchy or communism. It would lead in both cases to the abolition of the one social restraint by which he lives—private property. At a certain stage of the Revolution he is therefore forced to hold it back and support a counter-revolution in order to prevent the peasantry (as Luther in Germany), or the petty bourgeoisie (as in the Restoration of Charles II), or the proletariat (as the Thermidorians in France) from throwing off their chains. He is forced to go back on his nominal programme, and maintain the coercive, centralised State and the authoritarian Church in order to maintain the basis of his class. This results in all the illogical and bastard varieties of reformist Christianity which sprang into being with every stage of the bourgeois revolution. Catholicism alone remains 'pure', as the expression of the land-owning and primarily peasant-exploiting ruling classes, in Spain, Italy, South America and France, or, alternatively, as the religion of those exploited classes, even under bourgeois rule, who are exploited as peasants. To such, Catholicism, with its inverted world of rich dreams to make up for the real misery of the peasant's world, is the necessary religion and, as in Ireland, will appear to express their interests as against a bourgeois imperialist class. Catholicism is the religion of the special misery of the peasant and also of the rule of the landowners, just as Protestantism is the religion of the misery of the 'free' labourer and also of the rule of the bourgeois. The glories and richly populated heaven of the Catholic reflect the meaner, barer world of the peasant, just as the sterner heaven of the Protestant symbolises the less degraded existence of the exploited proletariat.

The 'logical' end of the bourgeois religion was Deism. The bourgeois class was a class which denied social relations and, in doing so, necessarily denied all the symbolisations of social relations in religion. Hence the Reformation demanded the sweeping away of Purgatory, of the saints, of all rites and ceremonies. Only the Spirit, indwelling in man, was left in Puritanism. This Spirit itself was simply the symbol of Will as the bourgeois believes it to be—spontaneous, free, and undetermined.

Religion, however also symbolised man's relations to Nature through society. In so far as the social forces of society—symbolised by God—are not all powerful, but meet with checks and must obey 'natural' laws, there seems something behind God, something greater than man's idealisation of human will, and this more powerful system is regarded as Fate, or God's own edict which he will only occasionally disobey by working miracles.

Now this order in nature is unfolded to view by man's very interpenetration with nature. Hence the superior technical efficiency of bourgeois economy, beginning with Galileo and da Vinci, generated an increasingly over-riding conception of this Fate or of God's unchangeable Will which, as more and more was learned about it, seemed more and more impersonal, empty, and mechanical. Via Descartes, Newton, Hobbes and the Encyclopaedists, this Fate became a transparent Deism which was almost indistinguishable from mechanical materialism, and became completely atheistic at the most revolutionary period of bourgeois struggle.

This itself was an expression of the bourgeois revolutionary movement. For it the world is automatic and mechanical —the problem of life is not in society but in the environment. All social restraints must therefore be removed to permit the maximum utilisation, investigation and exploitation of the environment, i.e., of property. This attitude to God and Nature became a charter of bourgeois revolution.

Such a movement inevitably meant that the propertyless exploited class, the proletariat, whose help was always demanded by the bourgeois in their revolutions, wanted to go still further, and abolish the social restraint of property which, by holding them in bondage, by arbitrarily and non-scientifically carving up the environment, denied the bourgeoisie's own slogan: 'Liberty, Equality and Fraternity.'

In practice therefore the bourgeoisie drew back before Deism and from 1793 to 1936 there was a series of retreating movements resulting in the maintenance of some kind of Church or official church theology which was arbitrary and coercive, just as the bourgeois State in spite of its democratic slogans was arbitrary and coercive—because the restraint of property could only be maintained arbitrarily and coercively. It became generally accepted that some religious instruction was "good" for the people. Thus, although already riddled with bourgeois criticism, religion was officially maintained by the bourgeois class, even though they themselves only partially or prevaricatingly believed in it.

This was accompanied later by a similar retreat in science. The recognition of the determined nature of the environment should have resulted in a recognition of the true nature of that determinism in society as a whole. This would have meant the destruction of the fundamental bourgeois position: that unsocialised bourgeois property is justified because the bourgeois will is free in itself, the sole active centre in society. Acceptance of this determinism would have led, not only to the 'naturalisation' of humanity but also to the 'humanisation' of nature, which in the bourgeois scheme is mechanical empty of human values and Newtonian. Instead of accepting this interpenetration, which would have involved the rejection of the bourgeois illusion, bourgeois theory swung over to the projection of the bourgeois human (not the scientific human) into nature. This led, as we show more fully in the essay, *Reality*, to absolute Idealism, which marked the final stage of coercive bourgeoisdom—the arbitrary Prussian State, with its negation of bourgeois theories of freedom; a State which was yet maintained by the imperative needs of bourgeois private property. In such a State a Professor could be dismissed after writing a simple book on ethics, by a decision of the Prussian Minister of Education which stated: 'that it was not a single passage which had given offence but the whole Scheme, and that a philosophy which did not deduce everything from the

Absolute could not be considered to be a philosophy at all.' The Absolute thus revealed itself in the rôle it was to play thereafter—the absolute demand that the State should protect private property and express the interests of the ruling class, even if it means war, economic disaster, and starvation, a demand that makes the guardian of private property seem to tower above society as the totalitarian State.

Thus the final disintegration of bourgeois culture is an elaborate phenomenon. The Will of God or Fate has, by the increasing technical achievement of the bourgeois, become causality, but only as applied to non-living matter, for the bourgeois cannot admit himself to be a determined individual—to do so would be to uncover the determining relations which are all social relations. The consciousness of these determining relations is simply Marxism, the world view of the revolutionary proletariat. Thus the bourgeois reserves for himself an area of spontaneity or non-causality in all values in which the human mind is concerned, and since there is no determinism there, they are all arbitrary and might be anything. This is expressed in some such formula as 'Science leaves man free to believe what he will.' 'Science applies to a different sphere from that of religion.'

Precisely because the development of bourgeois culture is the development of individualistic anarchy, religion has ceased to-day to be the expression of a coherent economy and becomes mere individualism. For this reason religion has become something widely abstracted from the concrete existence of men—at the opposite pole from the indwelling magic of the primitive, permeating all social life. The disintegration of bourgeois culture is marked by the appearance of thousands of different religions, systems of belief and idealistic philosophies—theosophy, spiritualism, Oxford Groupism, psycho-analysis (in its mystical form), Anthroposophy, and also all the varieties of belief that have sprung up within the nominal framework of one religion such as English Protestantism. These religions are all alike in that on the one hand, by their exaltation of the freedom and spontaneity of the spirit, they give a wish-fulfilment consolation to the hard-pressed human creature helpless as never before in the blind grip of an anarchic society; and, on the other hand, by their detachment of human values from material, by their idealism, by their denial of science and determination in all important spheres, they help to maintain things as they are, and struggle against any attempt of man to acknowledge and control the material forces of society. Thus the very disintegration of religion into all forms of mysticism and idealism, while it reflects the demoralisation of the society that produces this, by no means brings about an automatic collapse into rationality. On the contrary, this very disintegration and mysticism, this haze of bewilderment and cross-purposes, serves as a conservative force and a barricade of counter-revolution. To the counter-revolution every second gained is precious, however it is gained. All obstructions are aids and all haze or darkness valuable. The struggle against the real material misery of the world that produces this ideological haze must be an active struggle not merely to shatter existing society but to seize its forms and transform them; not merely to deny existing bourgeois ideology but to fuse its shattered fragments and use their content for a further ideological advance. It is not a question of posing religion against atheism; it is a question of turning an anarchic, neurotic society into an organised and sane one. This is a revolutionary task.

Beneath the ideological haze is an iron core, the maintenance by force of outworn social relations, the maintenance of bourgeois private property. This was only secured by the creation of the coercive State, and, as the revolt against capitalism grows stronger, so the State emerges as more absolute, coercive, and irrational. It becomes the Moloch to which decency, humanity, even religion itself must be sacrificed, not for any reason given but as an Absolute Imperative behind which we must not look, for if we look behind it we shall find the simple claim to profit. It is just this Absolute which symbolises the bourgeois right to property which now—no longer based on logic, reason or convenience—becomes a new God, a God of Force and Hate.

This new religion of bourgeois decadence is Imperialism, the patriotism of the monopoly stage of capitalism. The State comes first, all must be sacrificed to the interests of the nation, including the lives of other nations and the health and happiness of one's own people. Because the bourgeois property interests are interests now sharply opposed to those of the people as a whole, these interests and this State now separate themselves from the people and appear as Divine and Sacred entities whom to deny or attack is wicked, a blasphemy beyond the blasphemy of religion. Religions dating from early periods of capitalist development, before the coming of monopoly, find their symbolisations to be in conflict with the Moloch, and thus we find ranged against the State, and its absolute claim to enforce the naked property right of the bourgeois, large strata of the people still professing the old bourgeois religions, as well as the class-conscious proletariat. This Moloch patrotism, born during the jingo period of British Imperialism and in the Prussian State, reached a new height during the1914-18 War, and has received its final expression in Fascism. Against Fascism therefore appears a United Front of the proletariat supported by many Christians—the past and the future both edhying the outrageous present. In that struggle ideology is transformed and religion—in the actual struggle shedding its illusions one by one—finds its fantastic reality sucked into material reality, and its inverted world stood on its feet. It emerges as the self-feeling of a man who has found himself in society—as the consciousness of a classless society.

The passage from which sentences are quoted on pp. 17-19 is given in full below.

'The man who has found in the fantastic reality of heaven, where he sought a supernatural being, no more than his own reflection, will no longer be satisfied to find only the semblance of himself, only the unhuman, where he seeks, and must seek, his true reality.

'The basis of irreligious criticism is: Man makes religion, religion does not make man. And, in truth, religion is consciousness of self and the self-feeling of a man who has not yet found himself or has lost himself again. Also, man is not an abstract being existing outside the world. Man—that is, the world of men, the State, society. This State, this society, produces religion—an inverted consciousness of the world—because the world itself is an inverted world. Of *this* world religion is the general theory, its encyclopædic compendium, its logic in popular thought, its spiritual point d'honneur, its enthusiasm, its moral sanction, its solemn completion, its universal ground for truth and justification. It is the imaginary realisation of the human essence, necessary because the human essence has no true reality. The struggle against religion is therefore, indirectly, the struggle against that world whose spiritual aroma is religion.

'Religious misery is at once the expression of real misery and a protest against that real misery. Religion is the sigh of the hard-pressed creature, the heart of a heartless world, the spirit of unspiritual conditions. It is the opium of the people.

'The removal of religion as the illusory happiness of the people is the demand for their real happiness. The demand that they should give up illusions about their real conditions is the demand that they should give up the conditions which make illusion necessary. Criticism of religion is therefore at heart a criticism of the vale of misery for which religion is the promised vision.

'Criticism has torn away the imaginary flowers with which his chains were decked, not in order that man should wear his chains without the comfort of illusions, but that he may throw off the chains and pluck the living flowers. Criticism of religion disillusions man so that he may think, act and shape his reality as one who is disillusioned and come to full understanding, so that he may move on his own axis and thus be his own sun. Religion is but the false sun which revolves around him while he is not yet fully aware.

'Thus it is the *function of history*, after the *other-worldly truth* has collapsed, to establish *this world's truth*. Then, it is the *function of philosophy*, in the service of history, having destroyed the supernatural semblance of man's self-alienation, to go on and destroy the secular form of this self-alienation. Criticism of heaven thus turns into criticism of the world, *criticism of religion* into *criticism of law*, and *criticism of theology* into *criticism of politics*.'*

* Karl Marx: *Introduction to a Critique of Hegel's Philosophy of Law.*

II

BEAUTY

A Study in Bourgeois Æsthetics

WHAT is beauty? Is it a subject for discussion at all? Can it be defined in such a way as to provide a foundation for æsthetics? Is it a product of art? Or of nature?

To define: to limit the boundaries, to give an outline to the defined thing. Beauty, then, is defined by all that is not-beauty. This not-beauty circumscribes, limits, and defines beauty. But beauty is not opposed by not-beauty; it is opposed by ugliness. Yet the recognition of ugliness itself involves an æsthetic 'faculty', and sensibilities responding both to beauty and ugliness; and it is not possible to say where one begins and the other ends. Ugliness itself is an æsthetic value: the villain, the gargoyle, the grotesque, the Caliban, the snake-headed Furies, the triumph of Time's decaying hand, all these qualities interpenetrate with beauty, and help to generate and feed it. All live in the same world. Nowhere can we draw a distinct line and say, on this side lives the beautiful, and on that the ugly. All man's experience, all the rich complexity of his sculpted, painted, written art forms, all the elaborate multiform crowd of living animals and varied scenery, deny such a simple dichotomy. All form one world even if it contains opposites, and therefore the generating forces must lie at a lower level. Beauty and ugliness, the noble and the petty, the sublime and the ridiculous, all these opposite terms, *when used in an æsthetic way*, involve each other, and must be determined by other, different qualities, from which they spring.

We do not respond to all beautiful things in precisely the same way. The peculiar qualities of each thing colour the emotion we feel with an individual unique shade. If it were not so, the one beautiful thing would suffice; the one vase, painting, mountain would always be the sufficient stimulus to our emotion. This is not so. Yet of course there must be a likeness in all our responses for us to group them as one, as *æsthetic*.

Still more striking is the change in the responses to the beautiful from age to age. No age is satisfied wholly with the beautiful things of its forefathers, but produces other things, to the measure of its desires, quite clearly different from those beautiful traditions it inherits. This new vision does not exclude the old, however. The old still seems beautiful, but now its qualities are seen through a kind of mist or aerial perspective of intervening time, changing and toning its hues. The old beauty has been gathered up in the new. And that age which is least able to rest content with the beautiful things of the past, that creates things beautiful to its eyes most different, most revolutionary and most insurgent, is precisely that age which seems to us most in possession of beauty. We value the revolutionary, dissatisfied art works of the Renaissance, and see nothing in those of the Hellenising classicists or tired formalists who mechanically repeat the beautiful things of times gone by.

Man remains throughout this period much the same, but the changing pageant of his art, his poetry, and his buildings proclaims that at no stage does his idea of beauty remain constant, but continually demands expansion and rejection. All contents of the habitable world, of the known cosmos even, come to share in this strange irradiation. The rich

Americas, the glassy depths of the 'deep abyss', the spiral nebulæ, new birds and insects, jungles and swamps, the silent Poles and the breathless Equator, acquire for man's eyes with each generation a novel æsthetic quality and become things of a nature undreamt of before this time.

Remembering this, we start to define Beauty. The man looks at an object and calls it beautiful. This is a relationship repeatable by this one man with perhaps thousands of objects. What does it involve—what, in this subject-object relation, is the Beauty?

It must be, not in one relation but in all relations of man to object where man says: 'This is Beautiful'. It must be, therefore, something common to all beautiful objects and to all men finding an object beautiful.

The simplest answer is to say that the man is common to all objects, and therefore beauty is 'in' the man. Beauty is a state of the man. To the bourgeois æsthete this very simple solution of the problem seems so obvious that he has no patience with anyone who can think anything else. This is the solution advanced by I. A. Richards and C. K. Ogden:

'Beauty is attributed to objects which produce coenæsthesia.' *

The common term linking these relations wherein the man says 'This is beautiful' is therefore his 'coenæsthesia'. Here is a common term of the kind we sought for when we sought for something similar in all relations of men finding objects beautiful. Here then is a definition for beauty. Beauty is coenæsthesia.

Coenæsthesia is a wide term, and really includes the totality of proprioceptive impressions as far as they give rise to affects. Most neurologists picture the process as one in which interoceptive stimuli—particularly visceral stimuli—

* v. The Meaning of Meaning by I. A. Richards & C. K. Ogden.

give rise, *via* thalamic activity, to colorations of the conscious field known as feelings. Now it is quite plain that although the æsthetic emotions are coenæsthetic in this sense simply because they are affective, all coenesthetic sensations are not sensations of the beautiful. That would be to say that all feelings of pleasure or unpleasure are feelings of the beautiful. Consequently the definition of Richards and Ogden is inadequate. A pork chop, well done, may arouse strong feelings of coenesthesia, but it is not beautiful—or hideous. As an æsthetic object, it is neutral.

Why do the authors then arrive at this definition? It is in fact a typically bourgeois definition; beauty is a state of the bourgeois. This is not very different from many other bourgeois propositions springing out of the decay of bourgeois philosophy after Hegel, shown by the rise of positivism. In the same way Truth becomes an *economical* method for the bourgeois of describing phenomena. Causality becomes the way it *suits* the bourgeois to think of phenomena. And so on. It is the product of a 'tired' philosophy.

The definition of beauty as coenæsthesia is the ultimate product of mechanical materialism, of a philosophy that defines the environment as 'all that is not the bourgeois', while the Bourgeois stands outside it free and separate. The world thus becomes divested of all values arising from the relation of bourgeois to environment, for all such values, since they contain the bourgeois, are abstracted from the environment, for otherwise they would tie him to it. Such a non-valued environment ultimately contains nothing knowable and contains therefore nothing at all, but by the time this is discovered bourgeois culture is in such an advanced stage of disintegration that it seems immaterial whether the world is a real, coloured, qualified world or a ghostly ballet of equations.

(i) If on the one hand the environment is robbed of all

values in which it shares, the bourgeois is presented with all such values. They are his. Beauty is *in him*. But it is soon found that this by no means aggrandises such values.

For what is the bourgeois, according to the mechanical materialist? A body, a group of electrons, a collection of blood, bones, and neurones, subject to physiological laws, conditioned reflexes, and 'instincts'. Beauty and all similar values thus become physiological activity. Having dissolved the environment into moving molecules, atoms, ultimately into tensors and moved all values into the bourgeois, this type of bourgeois philosopher now starts to operate on the bourgeois himself. He also is the environment to other bourgeois; he also is matter. Therefore all the accumulation of values stripped from the environment and concentrated in him can now themselves quickly be shown to be nothing but physiological functions, biochemical and electronic phenomena—mere tensors.

This is the bourgeois nightmare of a predetermined Universe which includes the bourgeois, from which he shuddered away into absolute idealism.

(ii) If we start from the other end, with the mind as primary, all qualities which partake of the environment are stripped from mind. Applied to relations of the beautiful, this involves that the singularities of the beautiful objects, due to the way in which they differ among themselves, are to be abstracted from these relations in order to discover the essentially beautiful. The liquid eyes of the deer, the massive solidity of the mountain, the fatness of Falstaff, the coldness of an iceberg are qualities not common to mind but peculiar to the objects on which mind rests. They must all be stripped away and finally, by removing all environmental individualities from beauty as it inheres in beautiful relations, we are left with absolute Beauty, the Idea or concept of Beauty, which is homogeneous and bare of individualities, and is therefore completely mental.

But the objects of beauty vary from generation to generation of men, and appear to have existed before men exist. There is therefore a Beauty which is independent of the brain. Thus we get the absolute Idea of Beauty existing apart from the brains of men. This is that 'Beauty' of which æstheticians talk; meaning nothing but an Idea, something colourless, a kind of vague white-robed bare-footed personification going about the world. Such an idea is parasitic, because it sucks an emotive colouring from all beautiful objects, and yet has denuded those objects of just that in them which was the source of our delight—their self-hood and individuality. It is death to Art, because in the artist's flair for the difference, for the newness, for the intrinsic and peerless individuality of the beautiful object lies his power to make new beauty. It is equally deadening to the lover of beauty, for he loves beautiful *objects*—the daffodil, the Cézanne—*for themselves*, not because in them is a manifestation of an Idea of the Beautiful. Thus, when the extremes of bourgeois idealism and bourgeois mechanical materialism in the realm of Value are reached, there is not so much difference after all—to both Beauty dissolves and becomes something homogeneous, empty, dead—coenæsthesia or the Absolute Idea.

* * * * *

It is true of course that coenæsthesia enters into the beautiful relation, just as a neuronic wave of potential difference enters into the perceptual relation. How much is there to this side of the story?

Let us pick out at random a few generalised qualities and values:

Heat,	Cold,	Glory,	Happiness,
Pleasure,	Beauty,	Fear,	Pain.

All these may be regarded as affective: Man feels happy, pleased, afraid, feels pain, fear, that a thing is hot, that a thing is beautiful. But of course, in the way these feelings arise, each expresses a relation of the man to his environmental relation. *Something* makes man happy, he finds *something* to be pleasant. Yet there is plainly a difference in man's use of these concepts. Happiness, fear, pain and heat are all the accompaniment of nervous disturbances, are all in possession of a common physiological term. We locate happiness *in ourselves*, and this we do also with fear and pain, and yet we locate heat and beauty *out there*, in the object.

We locate it as the outcome of our experience. Take the concept of happiness. Experience shows us that certain objects in certain cases are associated with happiness, in the other cases with not-happiness. We find that movement away from those objects to others does not necessarily mean the removal of unhappiness. We find that happiness has a persistent quality through a large number of different 'I' environmental situations. Happiness is common to these situations. So is the 'I'. The environment is not common, but changes in these situations; so we locate happiness in the 'I'. A happy person is therefore to us a person who has *in him* happiness.

But fear, or joy, while showing a certain congruity in changing environmental situations, also show a certain incongruity. We may indeed find fear and joy persisting in certain changes, but we may find a given situation, particularly with fear, forcibly and abruptly changing the stability of the ego, from happiness or boredom to fear. Therefore we conceive fear and joy, as *a* fear and *a* joy, separate and impersonal, situated neither in the environment nor ourselves, but abruptly breaking in on both.

A pain we locate in ourselves but yet as something alien

to us which has gained a seat in us. This concept is necessitated by our experience (*a*) that we act immediately by withdrawing our bodies from the environment (therefore pain is alien, imposed on us by the environment), (*b*) that often pain cannot be so diminished but is still, after such actions, present in our bodies, as for example a toothache, or the pain of a wound after the blow. (Therefore pain is inside us.)

Heat and cold we locate entirely in objects because experience has shown us that movements of our body always remove us from the source of heat or cold. It is therefore not in ourselves, but the environment. In the sum of ego-environment relations, *happiness* vanished while the environment *remained* but *heat* vanished when the environment *changed.* Hence, just as happiness is located in the ego, heat is located in the environment.

Finally beauty, like heat, and unlike pain, fear, joy, pleasure or happiness is located entirely in the environment. The object is beautiful; we ourselves do not feel beautiful when we see a beautiful object.

In other words, it is man's experience that beauty is an objective quality—not wholly objective, because it is a relation between subject and object—but objective in the way that heat is. Like heat, beauty appears or disappears in man's conscious field according as he moves towards or from the beautiful object in his environment. the object itself remaining unchanged during this process. That is what men have felt when they called Beauty timeless, eternal, Divine. But we have already seen that to accept this, to separate the lover of beauty from beautiful objects, is to make Beauty either a colourless Idea or a physiological disturbance.

We find men agree about what is hot and what is cold in all ages. Moreover we can correlate differences of heat with differences of molecular movement and with the temperature of man's blood, above which temperature all seems 'hot' and below which, all seems 'cold'. By inference, we hold that these molecular movements with which heat is identified were the same in character long before man existed. This gives heat, in all its degrees, an objective existence independent of man. It is now described or compared with other qualities, (motion) more or less independently of the sensory nerves.

But we do not find men agreeing about what is beautiful in all ages. We find on the contrary that in each age:

(*a*) Men pick out different objects as beautiful, or pick out different aspects or details of objects already recognised as beautiful, for praise.

(*b*) Men not only pick out different objects as beautiful (beauty in nature) but make different beautiful objects (beauty in art) from age to age.

(*c*) Usually, however, the objects that earlier generations found or made beautiful, are accepted by later generations as beautiful, and the role of the later generation is that of either adding to them by enriching our perception of them, or subtly modifying our appreciation of their qualities.

We cannot find any non-æsthetic qualities in terms of which beauty can be exactly described independently of man, although we can find non-thermal qualities in terms of which heat can be exactly described. Thus we cannot infer back to describe the beauty of the world before man came into existence; we can only suppose that, 'if man could see such a world, he would find it beautiful'. But, to do so, we must imagine the observer already there; ourselves looking at such a world; we cannot imagine the world as a ballet of impersonal equations with the beauty expressed by these equations, as they express the heat of molecular movement.

How are we to reconcile the fact that we regard beauty,

unlike happiness, as a property of the environment, with our failure to produce comparative environmental qualities, as we can in the case of heat, which would suffice to determine it independently of man? We could only reconcile it if there were a triadity in the subject-object relation of man to beautiful object; if in addition to naked subject and naked environment, we had a third mediating term, something which remained unchanged while the subject changed and so could stand to it as environment and account for our projection of Beauty outside ourselves, and yet which changed while the bare environment remained unchanged, which would account for the historic change in what particular objects are found to be lovely or made beautiful.

We have actually such a third term; we have already referred to it; it is men as opposed to man—society. The *man* as born, as innate, uneducated and 'wild', changes little in the course of history, but of course he does not span all human history; only *men*-in-society does that. So in commenting on the change in man's estimation of beauty from age to age, we have already in fact admitted society as the cause of change in beauty, of the coming into being of new beauty. In commenting on the constancy of the environment throughout, we have in fact admitted that the objective environment in which beauty is situated is social rather than natural. If it were the unchanging environment in which beauty was situated, how could it change? If man, substantially unchanging in his innate make-up, faced the unchanging earth and stars without material mediation, how could an ever-changing beauty be generated? But man sees nature through social spectacles. 'Spectacles' is a partly incorrect analogy, for man is a part of society, and nature is a part of society. Society is a genuine middle term. To an individual man society stands as environment, and is included with the sun, earth and air. To nature, however, society stands as an active human force. The antimonies of beauty as a value can therefore only be resolved by regarding it as a social product, something secreted in the process of society. In the process of society, all nature enters. Man measures himself against infinite space, and takes his time from the sun. He feels the hot breath of the desert in his cities, and he goes out alone or in bands to establish himself in the jungles. He moves on the face of the lonely sea in man-made ships. The threads of social process penetrate, under the hands of Einstein and Amundsen, Freud and Rutherford, Kepler and Magellan, into remoter and remoter cracks of reality. The labouring masses of society root deep in the face of the earth. The farmer sowing the fruitful prairies, the lone hunter in untamed woods, and the sailor on the 'wine-dark' sea are all parts of the social process. As such, the social process generates everywhere beauty, not as a universal but as a specific social product, just as it generates science, politics, or religion.

We referred to the possibility of expressing heat in terms of other, non-sensory, qualities, so that heat had an objective metrical scale, correlated to but independent of man's experience. If it were possible completely so to describe heat, we should be discovering a self-contained, self-determined world. The complete goal is impossible. The completely non-human self-determined world of physics does not exist. There is something in heat as felt which can only be expressed in terms of the observer. But none the less such feeling, in its degree and appearance, can be completely *determined* by other qualities. Bourgeois philosophy attempts to close one world or the other, to make heat objective or mental. Dialectical materialists refuse to do this. Heat is determined by objective qualities but its appearance contains a newness, something peculiar to it as an event.

This is equally true of beauty. Beauty is determined by other non-æsthetic qualities, which account for its appearance and disappearance, its change and development. These qualities are not, as in the case of heat, kinetic, but sociological, they arise from the interaction of systems of men with the environment, in the course of labour processes. Such sociological qualities are not æsthetic: there is a distinct realm of æsthetics. Beauty can only be known, felt or described in the experience, and the experience is real, it is not a chance iridescence on the surface of atomic clouds, but a real intense property of the Universe. A man who had never felt heat would never be able to imagine it from a study of the kinetic theory of heat, however familiar he was with motion. A man who had never seen beautiful things would never know beauty, however complete his sociological data. Beauty is social. It is objective because it lives apart from me, in society. The smile of a Polycletan Hermes has qualities, not only in me, but in the Hellas which produced it, and all that has happened since and before to man. It is not, however, merely resident in society considered as a group of men. It stretches into all parts of the Universe because society, as active subject, is related to all other reality as object.

Happiness is not a social product, any more than a man is a social product. It is true that happiness arises out of the relation of me to my environment; my experience generates it. But it is like my flesh, instinctive and unsophisticated. It is like sorrow, anger and love, a quality which is as yet untransformed by society and is born the same in each man. It is genotypical. I, as individual subject, generate it in relation to the environment, as object. It is not independent of the environment, any more than my body is in its health. But happiness is not a social product any more than illness, which is produced by the environment, is a social product.

We need not suppose it will always be so. A day may come when man, become increasingly conscious of himself, may be able to make happy things, a happy environment, as he makes a beautiful thing. Happiness will then seem to him like beauty, not in himself but in his environment. He will be the creator, not the slave, of happiness and sorrow, as he is now the creator of beauty and ugliness. Then perhaps happiness will seem higher than beauty, or perhaps it will seem as if beauty, by a simple expansion, has taken up happiness within itself, and it is still beauty, but a larger, more universal beauty which we serve, a happiness which we now consciously create and actually see.

Beauty is not alone in playing a dual role as object to the individual and subject to the environment. Morality and goodness are the same; they are conceived of as greater than man and outside him, and yet change with society and are not expressible except in sociological terms. God as he appears in all myths, religions and metaphysics, is such a value. Just as Beauty, imagined as a real indwelling goddess, ceased to exist at a certain stage in social development, and yet beauty the objective value persisted, so God, conceived as a person, to-day ceases to exist, and yet morality and goodness, as objective values outside the individual, persist. Both are social products. Truth is another such value. We cannot conceive truth apart from a true statement—something human, and yet we know that truth is not just what I, the individual, think to be true. Truth is a social product; it is a particular relation of the individual, *via* society, to the rest of the Universe.

But truth, goodness, and beauty are not 'just' social products. Their specific social rôles, in which man as individual, men as society, nature as environment and reality as including individual and society and environment, all figure, differ among themselves and generate their peculiar quality. What is this peculiar quality in the case of beauty? Beauty tells us something, not as a statement tells us something, but as a glance tells us something. It is the apprehension of a genuine quality. A beautiful thing has a significant content, just as a true statement has. But it is not the same significance. What is this difference between true statements and beautiful things?

In the course of the contact of the individual with reality, he experiences various emotions. These emotions, or affects, are new qualities. Instinct is what we call a simple repetition of hereditary habits, the mechanical reappearance of the old. Such simple responses to external or internal stimuli change from age to age, but, in relation to the rapid tempo of social life, there is a consistency about them which leads us to separate them as hypothetical entities, the instincts. Situations which, while evoking instinctual responses, do not permit their emergence unchanged, but cause a suspension or interruption of the pattern, produce affects or emotions. The result of such a situation is the transforming, or conditioning (Pavlov), repression or sublimation (Freud) of the response. Thus the affects or emotions are the sign at once of an instinctive response and of its change in a certain *situation* or subject-object pattern.

The instincts as mechanical responses are unconscious. It is consciousness itself—a particular group of innervations and their relation to reality—which calls them 'unconscious'. What it means by this term is: 'not included with us'. But all innervations, being innervations of one nervous system, are related. Thus even the unconscious group, those innervations 'not included with us', are in indirect connexion with the conscious group. In so far as they leave mnemic traces, unconscious innervations can be known by consciousness. The nature of this 'unconscious' excluded group is such that they leave crude mnemic traces but, once left, these traces are enduring. Unconscious 'memories' are simple, poor, and permanent; conscious memories are subtle, rich, and fluid.

Affects are conscious. A feeling is felt. But the affects, the emotions, emerge as a specific relation between a situation and an innate response. The relation between situation and response generates these emotions. Consciousness is a relation of two unconscious terms, body and environment.

The organism encounters situations through its exteroceptive neurones, through sight, hearing, touch, and smell, of which in man sight and hearing are dominant. The organism has responses because of innate potentialities buried in it, in its chromosomes, in its sympathetic and parasympathetic systems, in its visceral innervations. Of course there is no gulf between situation receptors and response-effectors. The eye itself has innate responses; and stimuli arise inside the organism. A stomach ache is a situation. But the *situation* is sensory, is *external*; the *response* is somatic, is *interior*.

An emotion which expresses a particular new relation between a situation and a response therefore has both a sensory component and a somatic component. It is not a mixture, it is a quality—a relation of two terms. The situation appears as the form: the present situation as a percept, sound heard, odour smelt or tactile sensation; the past situation as a memory. The response appears as the feeling content, as the fear, desire, or boredom associated with the presentation. Both are intimately mingled. In thought the situation appears as the memory-image, thought, dream and so forth, and the response as the feeling tone, or affective colouring of the thought. In reflection, affective tone and percept are more closely entwined, for whereas the organism is the same, there is no real situation 'outside-now'. The affect has almost sucked up into itself the sensory presentation; hence the possibility of imageless thought.

Thus all consciousness may be regarded as groups of entities which may be divided into feelings, the *content*; and situations being met or remembered, the *form*. Feelings are common to all contents, but the form is different for present and for past situations. The form of the one is a percept; of the second, a memory or thought. But the affect differs subtly according to whether the form is a memory or a percept.

A thing may be unconsciously perceived if it evokes no new response. It is habitual, always there; we do not notice it.

The field of consciousness therefore represents the ingression of the new into the organism-situation relation. The affective basis is the organismal basis and the thought or perceptual form is the situation form. But they completely interpenetrate; they are not separable. They determine each other. Each change in consciousness involves a change in the environment. Of course, for each component of consciousness, the change may be chiefly organismal or chiefly environmental. This difference of degree, which never proceeds so far as to enable us to call any component *absolutely* one or the other, is important. Too 'pure' a percept, or too 'deep' a feeling is in either case unconscious. It is not the purity or vividness of either that consciousness expresses, but a change in their relation, an impact of the two. Consciousness is therefore change, it is the ingression of the new. It is the seat or aggregation of the novelties in a man's relations with reality. Such new qualities clump to form a conscious field, as bacteria clump in serum. The field is not static; it grows, changes and expands. It is not self-determined; on the contrary the field is the expression of the determining relation between the organism and the rest of reality.

In examining these contents we may sort them so as to pay special attention to the *forms*, to the percepts and memories of situations encountered in reality, to the bits of reality apparently embedded in consciousness.

The study of consciousness then becomes a study of the bits of reality embedded in consciousness, or the portions of outer reality in the conscious field. There is a tendency to call the outer reality quite simply 'Reality', so that this sorting becomes the study of reality.

The objective of such a study is truth. It is the goal of science. In so far as the 'situation' portions of the conscious field separate themselves out, a greater and greater grip of reality is presumed to be obtained. Such a programme is of course the programme above all of 'physics'.

But just because all contents of the conscious field, in so far as they represent the ingression of the new into the subject-object relation, contain both emotion and percept, feeling and memory, it is never possible in fact to find a conscious quality which is all situation and bare of feeling. The following-out of the programme of physics therefore gradually strips the world of reality of all qualities in consciousness in which a feeling tone or 'subjective factor' is concerned. This means stripping the real world, the object of science, of all reality. It becomes simply a group of equations.

But equations are mental. They represent the laws of the comparison of qualities between themselves. Thus the real world becomes virtually nothing—unappetising and bare of interest. It becomes, finally, meaningless. Thus although science, alone of activities, has as its goal objective truth and the extracting from consciousness of the 'pure' situation elements, this will, if carried to its utmost extent, rob truth of truth. For truth implies some affective attitude, some relation of organism to environment, by which it is generated. Truth can never be a criterion of a complete system of metrics, considered as self-sufficient in themselves, for the circle of metrics is closed. They constitute a world in themselves. The only criterion here is consistency. The question we ask of metrics is: 'Is the world fully closed? Do we arrive back finally at our initial axioms?' Now this consistency is quite different from what we mean by truth, the goal of the scientist, which spurs him on in his arduous labour.

What then is this Truth? For what do we in fact search the field of consciousness in its name? The field of consciousness is not static, it is generated by change. Consciousness is the product or affective heat of a clash between the response of the organism and a situation to which the response is not exactly geared. The impact, changing both, is preserved in the organism's behaviour as a modification and in its consciousness as a feeling and a thought. This conscious field changes; it has its laws of flow and recombination. Man thinks, plans, wills, introspects. Consciousness is the continual ingression of the new. Consciousness is the sign of a behaviour modification. Man 'learns' by experience, by the ingression into his organism of the new. Consciousness is the result of interaction, and is a guide to action.

But action implies the organism. The organism acts. If consciousness is simply the individual's sum of behaviour modifications, available as a guide to fresh situations, if each impact changes organism and environment, truth is a criterion of action. A component of consciousness is only generated by a tension between response and situation which do not fit like hand in glove, and because there is a discrepancy there is energy, heat, perception, feeling, as the hand is forced into the glove and as a result hand and glove are both altered in shape. Truth then is given man in his attempt to change the world. In changing it, of course, he changes himself.

That is why science is never hypothesis alone. It is always hypothesis plus experiment. In the experiment there is a tension or contradiction between man's beliefs—the sum of his responses as a result of previous experience—and a given situation—the crucial experiment or discovery of a piece of reality which does not fit the response. As a result the hypothesis is changed. Man's consciousness is changed.

Hence science's history is a continual modification of hypothesis by experiment. As the result of each modification, man's relation to objective reality is changed—he alters from a being at the centre of the Universe to one on the limits of it, and then to a man in no absolute place. Truth always appears as a result of man's successful interaction with his environment. Always he can only find truth by changes and reality. By analysing, by setting up a mock world in the laboratory, by moving his position somewhere to view an eclipse, by making experiments in artificial lightning—in all such ways he changes reality, and all these are precursors to far vaster changes—bridges, ships, roads, tilled land. Each time, in altering reality, he generates new truth, and finds it only thus.

Hence, except in action, truth is meaningless. To attempt to find it in a mere scrutiny of the conscious field, by 'pure' thought, results not in truth but in mere consistency. The contents of the mind are measured against themselves without the incursion of a disturbance from outside, which disturbances in fact, in the past history of the field, are what have created it. Since innumerable consistent worlds are possible, there would be as many criteria of reality as there were people with different conscious experiences.

But action upon nature demands co-operation if it is to be fully effective. The organism which will be most in possession of truth, which will most deeply penetrate and widely change the environment, will be an organism able to co-operate with other organisms in that change. The very combination, by division of labour, produces a qualitative change. What millions of organisms do separately is nothing compared to what they can do in co-operation to a common goal. Truth appears as an outcome of the labour process, for it is the labour process that demands and at the same time dictates the co-operation of organisms.

Thus a mediating term now appears in truth, which we first analysed as an outcome of the bare organism faced by bare environment. But now the bare organism faces society and its culture, and the bare environment faces, not the lone organism, but the tremendous apparatus of co-operating men.

In fact this occurred from the very beginning. The labour process itself generates the co-operation which changes and expands the responses of the organism, and gives rise to sufficiently many new situations to make it possible to talk of 'truth'. From the very start the labour process, by the society it generates, acts as a mediating term in the production of truth.

From the very start the labour process gives rise to material capital. Simple enough at first, taking the form of mere tools, customs, magico-scientific objects, seeds, huts, these were yet all-important as the beginnings of culture. To our argument they bear this important relation, that all such enduring products represent social truths. The plough is as much a statement about the nature of reality as the instructions how to use it. Each is useless without the other; each makes possible the development of the other. All these social products are generated by the nature of reality, but their form is given by the organism in its interaction with reality. The nature of fields and plants imposes on the organisms specific types of co-operation in sowing and reaping and determines the shape of the plough. It imposes on them language, whereby they signify to each other their duties and urge each other on in carrying them out. Once established the labour process, extending as remotely as observation of the stars, as widely as organisation of all human relations, and as abstractedly as the invention of numbers, gathers and accumulates truth. Faster and faster it proliferates and moves. The bare organism is to-day from birth faced with an enormous accumulation of social truth in the form of buildings, laws, books, machines, political forms, tools, engineering works, complete sciences. All these arise from co-operation; all are social and common. Generated by this capital, truth is the past relation of society to the environment accumulated in ages of experience. It is actually created by the conflict of social organisms with new situations in the course of the labour process.

But the very richness and complexity of this 'frozen' truth, the very elaborateness of an advanced culture and a functioning society, ensures that the naked organism will be confronted with the greatest possible variety of 'situations' This will ensure the greatest possible activity of a man's consciousness, and the maximum of mutual transformation of his responses, his instincts, and the material environment. There will be a rapid ingression of newness. This itself will generate new truth. Man, as experiencing individual, will find himself constantly negating the truths given in his social environment.

Thus we see the cause of the apparent antinomies in truth. Truth appears to be in the environment, to be objective and independent of me. Yet the attempt to extract a completely non-subjective truth from experience produces only metrics. Moreover the environment changes only slowly, but the truth of science or reality as known to man, has changed rapidly.

Truth, then, is in my environment, that is, in my culture,

in the enduring products of the labour process. Thus truths, although similar in their lack of newness and fixation to my inherited responses, are yet different in that responses emerge from the unconscious, *inside* me, whereas the inheritances of culture come to me as 'situations', as things learned, taught, or told me, as experience, as *environment*. But I do not regard myself as bound to the social criteria of truth; on the contrary it is my task to change their formulations, where my experience contradicts them.

* * * * *

But, it will be urged, we were to discuss beauty, and now it is only truth we have obtained. Writing when bourgeois English poetry was at its height at the same time as bourgeois German philosophy was reaching its climax, Keats said:

> "Beauty is truth, truth is beauty"—that is all
> Ye know on earth, and all ye need to know.

A modern bourgeois poet, T. S. Eliot, has announced himself unable to understand these lines of Keats, just as modern bourgeois philosophers show themselves unable to understand Hegel's dialectics. But we saw that the pursuit of truth was the study of the objective elements in the conscious field. We saw further that completely objective elements could never be obtained. A world built up in such a way dissolved into mere metrics, and truth became consistency. To every percept and thought, an affect or subjective tinge inevitably attached itself. We never had a mere situation but always a response to a situation.

Thus truth never stands by itself as 'pure'. It is always generated in action, in instinctive organismal response going out into the situation and modifying both itself and the situation, begetting emotion as a result. Absolute, static, eternal truth is thus impossible.

But every such action involves a desire, a volition, aim, fear, disgust, or hope. Thus truth is always tinged with the subject and with emotion. This is not a discoloration. As we saw, any thoroughgoing attempt to wash truth clean of such affective discoloration simply washed the world away, for it becomes bare geometry. We do not feel ourselves passively responding to a situation, we feel active and subjective and seats of innovation. Necessarily so, because each transaction with a situation changes us, and therefore makes us a new centre of force. This is expressed directly in consciousness.

If we sort out of consciousness all the subjective elements we now orientate the same field *in an entirely different way*. The connection between conscious contexts is no longer outer reality, but the responses. We now group all the conscious contexts into like responses (love, fear, self-preservation). The laws of thought now become the laws of affective association. The affective association of ideas discovered by Freud, which threw a flood of light upon dreams, is not so much the discovery of a secret connexion as a law arising from our mode of analysis of conscious contents. If we sort them according to the responses or somatic components, we discover ideas to be affectively associated. If we sort them according to the situation or environmental components, we find them to be associated by contiguity and other laws taken from the environment. Both methods are equally correct. Both affect and thought, both response and situation, are given in the one conscious glow.

When we are concerned with dream and day-dream, attention is introverted; the body ceases to be closely concerned with the situation. The response or instinctive element in consciousness then becomes dominant. Hence the value of the Freudian or affective analysis of consciousness in such states. The 'deeper', and more somatic, the innervations, the more dominating becomes the response. The more external, and sensory the innervations, the more dominating becomes the situation. The environment rather than the instinct gives the main clue to the structure of the perceptual field; the response lays bare the secret structure of the phantastic field.

A development may take place. The body may be introverted, and unconcerned with its immediate environment, and yet it will not be dreaming, it will be thinking. It will be striving to mould its dream according to the nature of all past situations, according to its experience of outer reality. It will be attempting to realise the laws of outer reality, and penetrate its nature. This is science. It is a scientist thinking, however crudely, for there has been genuine synthesis between almost unconscious dream full of somatic drives and conscious perception, full of environmental shape. These have been fused in thought. Dream draws vividness and restraint from perception; perception gets a flexibility of recombination, an onward drive to a goal, from dream. The result is thought, as rational scientific thought.

But the same development leads to another. Behaviour is not only intra-somatic and conscious; it is also overt and visible in action. The organism is conscious, and is acted on by the environment, but it also behaves and acts on the environment. In its behaviour it is guided by perception, but perception cannot present it with a goal. Perception guides it but it is impelled by 'instinct'. The somatic element in consciousness now figures as a programme for change—what we 'want to do'. In trying to bring about our wishes, they too are transformed.

But perception is not 'pure' perception—perception *only* of the present situation. By introversion, by stiffening dream with the memories of past perceptions, perception has become 'rational' thought. Perception is widened into a general scheme of reality as experienced over a time. Reason, or congealed cognition, now guides instinct. In helping to change the environment, cognition too is modified and beeomes truer and subtler.

But how can I by myself effect more than the slightest change in my environment? I need the co-operation of other men. But this involves perceptions held in common: we must all have similar views of reality. Reason and perception therefore become social, become crystallised in languages, tools, techniques. This has the advantage that I can now draw not only on my brief experience of percepts, but on the combined and sifted experiences of thousands of generations, preserved in language, tool, or technique. This has become dominating. Even from the start it was so; man found himself, by the necessities of the labour process, sharing a common view of reality, and inheriting the seeds, experience, and advice of a preceding generation. Even before language, the labour process, if it involved only common hunting tactics not inherited but taught, would involve a common world-view however crude, and would generate a Truth resident not wholly in oneself but also in one's environment. Thus long before science has a name or a distinct existence, it is generated as a social product. Truth is created and extended before the concept could exist, as part of the labour process.

But the labour process, involving a social view of the necessities of the environment, a general consciousness in man of laws existing outside him in reality, involves also a social unity of response to these necessities and this environment. The interaction produces a change, and as the change becomes more willed, it generates increasing consciousness not only of the structure of reality but also of one's own needs. The goal is a blend of what is possible and what is desirable, just as consciousness is a blend of what is response and what is situation. Or, to be more precise, just as consciousness is the product of a tension between response and situation which do not precisely fit each other, so the goal is a product of a tension between what is possible and what is desirable. They are forced to meet; they are synthesised; and as a result both are changed, are fused into an attainable goal. Of all possibles and all desirables, the laws of reality enforce only one wedding, and the child is a new generation.

But if the desirable is to be held clearly in mind, if all action is somatically motivated, or *willed*, and therefore has an affective as well as a perceptual element—then there must be a community of desire as well as a community of perception. There must be a community of instinct, as well as a community of cognition. The heart, as well as the reason, must be social. The community must share a body in common, as well as an environment in common. Its hopes, as well as its beliefs, must be one. This hope, which is the opposite to science, we may call art. Just as Truth is the aim of science, Beauty is the end of art.

But both deflate abjectly if we attempt to isolate them. If we try to get them 'pure' we get nothing. Both are products of the living organism in the real world, and this means that every element is determined both by organism and environment.

We saw that the pursuit of Truth, and the separation of all environmental elements in the conscious field, produced not Truth but consistency. It produced an unreal dematerialised world, devoid of quality; in fact a mere series of equations. The pursuit of Beauty, and the separation of all affective elements in the conscious field, produces not Beauty but physiology. We get merely the body with its reactions.

But both Truth and Beauty are in fact generated already blended in action, in the social labour process visualised throughout human history. In this they are indivisible. Both continually play into each other's hands. Science makes the percepts, the possibilities, the world with which the body's desire concerns itself, continually richer and more subtle. Art makes the body's incursions into reality always more audacious, more curious, and more indefatigable.

Of course to the bourgeois with his ideal closed worlds, Truth and Beauty, art and science, appear not as creative opposites but as eternal antagonists. Even Keats who saw their kinship, could yet complain that science had robbed the rainbow of its beauty. This is because science and art, as long as they seem something distinct, situated in the environment entirely on the one hand (science) and in the heart entirely on the other (art), must seem exclusive and inimical. They seem to raise up two different worlds, of which we can choose one only. One is bare of quality, and the other is destitute of reality, so that we cannot rest easily on either horn of the dilemma. Only when we see that the separation is artificial and that response and situation are involved throughout consciousness and are part and parcel of the social process which generates both truth and beauty—only then can we see that there is no such deadly rivalry as we supposed but that on the contrary these opposites each create the other. The 'secret' connection between the two is the world of concrete society.

In all social products, therefore, affect and percept, response and situation, inevitably mingle. They do not merely mingle, they activate each other. In language every word has an affective as well as a cognitive value. The weight of each value varies in each case. Some words, such as interjections, are almost entirely affective. Others, such as scientific names, are almost entirely cognitive. But an entirely affective language—that is, sounds having only affective associations—ceases to be language. It becomes music. An entirely cognitive language—that is, sounds having only cognitive associations—also ceases to be a language; it becomes mathematics. In doing so, both seem to exchange rôles. Music no longer refers to outer reality; but it does not disappear into the body; it becomes for the body outer reality. For the body, listening to the music, the sounds are now environment; nothing is referred to. Mathematics, though it has no affective reference, does not disappear into the environment. On the contrary it becomes pure thought; it becomes the body operating on the environment. Cognition and affection can never be separated. The attempt to do so simply begets a new thing, in which they are united again.

Not only language but all social products have an affective role. Each society evolves its own gestures, deportment, and manners. These include a reference to reality, a pointing to something, the necessary opening of doors to get through them, or lifting of food to feed oneself, or moving of legs to get from one place to another. But these actions also include an affective element: all can be done 'beautifully' or artistically. One can point with an air, open a door politely, feed oneself quietly and 'off silver', walk slowly and with dignity. All this is beauty; all this is desirable; all this is a social product. Different societies have quite different notions of what is desirable in these things.

All objects, from a house to a hat, share these cognitive and affective elements. A hat has a real cognitive environmental function, so has a house. The hat must keep rain and sun off our heads; the house must keep out wind and weather, resist perhaps the robber and marauder. But both are modified by the affective element. The hat must add honour, dignity and grace to the head. The house must express respectability or power; and must contain rooms of a certain shape and size, because of the manners and social customs of the age.

Action designed only to express an affective purpose becomes, like music, an environment; dancing is a *spectacle*. Action designed only to express a cognitive purpose, and to achieve a goal which is not in itself really desired, becomes action in itself desirable, as in the mock-flights and trivial goals of sport, in which all energies are bent on securing something not really to be desired. Between sport and dancing stretch all the forms of action designed to secure an affective but real goal, that is, all forms of work, from sowing and reaping to factory production.

All forms of representation have the same duality. The faithful congruence of representation to reality, robbed of all affective elements, becomes not really a representation at all, but a symbol—the diagram. The attempt to make representation purely affective, without reference to environment, produces what is in itself an environment—the town and the building. Between lies the richness of pictorial illustration—the painting, the sculpture, the film, and the play.

In primitive civilisation this intimate generation of truth and beauty in the course of the labour process and their mutual effect on each other is so clear that it needs no elaboration. The harvest is work, but it is also dance; it deals with reality, but it is also pleasure. All social forms, gestures, and manners have to primitives a purpose, and are both affective and cognitive. Law is not merely the elucidation of a truth in dispute, but the satisfaction of the gods, of the innate sense of rightness in man's desires. Myths express man's primitive instincts and his view of reality. The simplest garment or household utensil has a settled beauty. Work is performed in time to singing, and has its own fixed ceremony. All tasks have their lucky days. Truth and beauty, science and art are primitive, but at least they are vitally intermingled, each giving life to the other.

It is the special achievement of later bourgeois civilisation to have robbed science of desirability and art of reality. The true is no longer beautiful, because to be true in bourgeois civilisation is to be non-human. The beautiful is no longer real, because to be beautiful in bourgeois civilisation is to be imaginary.

This itself is simply a product of the fundamental bourgeois position. Our own proposition about beauty is this: whenever the affective elements in socially known things show social ordering, there we have beauty, there alone we have beauty. The business of such ordering is art, and this applies to all socially known things, to houses, gestures, narratives, descriptions, lessons, songs and labour.

But to the bourgeois this proposition seems monstrous, for he has been reared on the anarchy of the social process. He refuses to recognise it. He recognises only one social process—commodity-manufacture, and one social tie—the market. The bourgeois produces for and buys from the market, governed as an individual by social relations masquerading as laws of supply and demand.

Thus any attempt at social consciousness which necessarily involves the manipulation of desires, *i.e.* of 'the laws' of supply and demand, seems to him outrageous. But this is just what art is—the manipulation or social ordering of desires, and therefore of the laws of supply and demand. Art gives values which are not those of the market but are use-values. Art makes 'cheap' things precious and a few splashes of paint a social treasure. Hence the market is the fierce enemy of the artist. The blind working of the market murders beauty. All social products, hats, cars, houses, household utensils and clothes, become in the main unbeautiful and 'commercialised', precisely because the maker in producing them does not consider social process, does not scheme how to order socially their affective values in accordance with their use, but merely how to satisfy a demand for them with the maximum profit to himself. This extends finally to those products which have no other purpose than affective ordering—paintings, films, novels, poetry, music. Because here too their affective ordering is socially unconscious, because it is not realised that beauty is a social product, there is a degradation even of these 'purest' forms of art products. We have commercialised art, which is simply affective massage. It awakens and satisfies the instincts without expressing and synthesising a tension between instinct and environment. Hence wish-fulfilment novels and films; hence jazz. The bourgeois floods the world with art products of a baseness hitherto unimaginable. Then, reacting against such an evident degradation of the artist's task, art withdraws from the market and becomes non-social, that is *personal*. It becomes 'highbrow' art, culminating in personal fantasy. The art work ends as a fetish because it was a commodity. Both are equally signs of the decay of bourgeois civilisation due to the contradictions in its foundation.

The ravages of bourgeois unconsciousness destroy not only the social product but the producer. Labour now becomes, not labour to achieve a goal and to attain the desirable, but labour for the market and for cash. Labour becomes blind and unconscious. What is made, or why it is made, is no longer understood, for the labour is merely for cash, which now alone supports life. Thus all affective elements are withdrawn from labour, and must therefore reappear elsewhere. They now reappear attached to the mythical commodity which represents the unconscious market—cash. Cash is the music of labour in bourgeois society. Cash achieves objective beauty. Labour in itself becomes increasingly distasteful and irksome, and cash increasingly beautiful and desirable. Money becomes the god of society. Thus the complete disintegration of a culture on the affective side is achieved, and has resulted from the same causes as its disintegration on the cognitive side.

Beauty, then, arises from the social ordering of the affective elements in socially known things. It arises from the labour process, because there must not only be agreement about the nature of outer reality, but also agreement about the nature of desire. This agreement is not static. In the social process, outer reality becomes increasingly explored, and this makes the social process more far-reaching and deeply entrenched in the environment, while each fresh sortie into reality alters the nature of desire, so that here, too, fresh integrations are necessary. This pressure, both in science and art, appears as an individual experience. A scientist inherits the hypotheses, and an artist inherits the traditions, of the past. In the scientist's case an experiment, and in the artist's case a vital experience indicates a discrepancy, a tension, whose synthesis results in a new hypothesis or a new art work. Of course the scientist feels the tension as an error, as something in the environment; the artist as an urge, as something in his heart.

* * * * *

Science and art, as we use them in current language, are more partial and restricted than in my use. Science, as generally used, involves not all the cognitive elements in the labour process but only the *new* elements. The scientist is on the border line where new hypotheses are generated to modify technique. In factory, in building, in housework, and all daily occupation, the cognitive elements are familiar and traditional. They are technique rather than science. The world-view is not expanding here; reality is as our fathers knew it; but the scientist is situated on the very expanding edge of the world-view. Here new regions are continually coming into sight; discrepancies in experience continually arise to make him modify yesterday's formulations. The same applies to the artist. In daily life, in manners, desires, morals, hopes and patriotisms we tread the daily round; we feel as our fathers do; but the artist is continually besieged by new feelings as yet unformulated, he continually attempts to grasp beauties and emotions not yet known; a tension between tradition and experience is constantly felt in his heart. Just as the scientist is the explorer of new realms of outer reality; the artist continually discovers new kingdoms of the heart.

Both therefore are explorers, and necessarily therefore share a certain loneliness. But if they are individualists, it is not because they are non-social, but precisely because they are performing a social task. They are non-social only in this sense, that they are engaged in dragging into the social world realms at present non-social and must therefore have a foot in both worlds. They have a specially exciting task, but a task also with disadvantages comparable to its advantages. The scientist pays for his new realms by travelling without affective companionship, with a certain deadness and silence in his heart. The artist explores new seas of feeling; there is no firm ground of cognitive reality beneath his feet; he becomes dizzy and tormented. Those not on the fringes of the social process get their life less new but more solid, less varied but more stable. Their values are more earthy, more sensuous, more mature. They are rooted, certain, and full. It is time for the antagonism between scientist and artist to cease; both should recognise a kinship, as between Arctic and tropical explorers, or between bedouins of the lonely deserts and sailors on the featureless sea.

But they must not suppose that a line can ever be drawn between science and other social cognition, and art and other social affection. The social process is far too closely woven for that. The ingression of new values takes place at all parts; only we call certain operations scientific or artistic because there we see the ingression most clearly. In education cognitive and emotional tradition is chiefly at work, but on the one hand even here there is an ingression of the new, and, on the other hand, the artist and the scientist are being educated as well as learning new things all their lives.

If they remember this, they will not make the mistake of supposing they are opposite poles, between which the whole social process is generated. This is to suppose profit produces capital. In fact profit is produced by capital, and yet continually augments it. Science and art represent the profit on social capital. They are pushed out into the deserts of the unknown by the very workings of society. They lead, but they were instructed; they find new worlds of life, but they were supported by the old. Always we find only terms drawn from the labour process to be adequate to describe their function, and only this can explain the nature of Beauty and Truth, how man can never rest on the truth his eyes tell him or the beauty his heart declares, but must go about finding new truth, and cannot rest until he has created wtih his hands a new beauty.

The artist takes bits of reality, socially known, to which affective associations adhere, and creates a mock world, which calls into being a new affective attitude, a new emotional experience. New beauty is thus born as the result of his social labour.

But if art works are artificial, and beauty is a social product, how do we find beauty in the natural thing, in seas, skies, a mountain, and daffodils?

To separate in this way natural things from artificial is to make as dangerous a distinction as that between environmental and affective elements in the conscious field, or between mental and material qualities. Society itself is a part of nature, and hence all artificial products are natural. But nature itself, as seen, is a product of society. The primitive does not see seas, but the river Oceanus; he does not see mammals, but edible beasts. He does not see, in the night sky, blazing worlds in the limitless void, but a roof inlaid with patines of bright gold. Hence all natural things are artificial. Does that mean that we can make no distinction between nature and art? On the contrary, we can clearly distinguish two opposites, although we must recognise their interpenetration. In all phenomena, from hats to stars, seasons to economic crises, tides to social revolutions, we can distinguish varying portions of change, varying portions of the ingression of the unlike. The most rapid evolution is that of human society, of its customs, towns and hand-made products. The next that of animals and plants. The next that of the solar system. The next that of our galaxy. The whole universe in fact changes, but it changes at different rates. The region of most change, human society, as it were, separates itself out from a background of least change, which we call 'nature'—stars, mountains and daffodils. The line can nowhere be precisely drawn; and in all cases it is man, a social product, confronting nature, and finding beauty in it. Nature finds no beauty in nature; animals do not look at flowers or stars. Man dies, and therefore it is the social process which has generated in him the ability to see beauty in flowers and stars. This ability changes in character. The sea is beautiful to a European, to an ancient Athenian, to a Polynesian islander, but it is not the same beauty; it is always a beauty rooted in their cultures. The frozen sea is to the Eskimo a different beauty from the warm sea of the Gulf; and the blazing sun of the Equator a different beauty from the faint six-months-dead sun of the Arctic.

Those elements in nature which are most universal and have changed least in the history of man, may be expected to produce, in interaction with him, the most constant quality. Hence we feel rightly that there is something simple, primitive, and instinctive in the beauty we see in certain primitive, simple things. This must never be pushed too far. The richest and most complex appreciation of natural beauty belongs to the civilised man, not to the primitive. We may oppose the art-work just made to the enduring mountain as an artificial to a natural beauty, but the difference is one of degree. In both cases beauty emerges as a quality due to a man, in the course of social process, gazing at a piece of his environment. The ancient town, with weathered walls, full of history and character, is a part of nature, and is yet a completely artificial product; the sun lights it and the wind weathers it. There is no dichotomy between nature and art, only the difference between pioneers and settled inhabitants.

Art, then, conditions the instincts to the environment, and in doing so changes the instincts. Beauty is the knowledge of oneself as a part of other selves in a real world, and reflects the growth in richness and complexity of their relations. Science conditions the environment to the instincts and in doing so changes the environment. Truth is the knowledge of the environment as a container for, and yet known by and partly composed of, one's own self and other selves.

Both are products of the labour process—that is to say, both are realised in action. Truth and Beauty are not the goals of society, for directly they become goals in themselves, they cease to exist. They are generated as aspects of the rich and complex flow of reality. The scientist or the artist is only a special kind of man of action: he produces truth or beauty, not as an end but as the colour of an act. Consciousness, society, the whole world of social experience, the universe of reality, is generated by action, and by action is meant the tension between organism and environment, as a result of which both are changed and a new movement begins. This dynamic subject-object relation generates all social products—cities, ships, nations, religions, the cosmos, human values.

Bourgeois culture is incapable of producing an Æsthetics for the same reason that most of its social products are unbeautiful. It is disintegrating, because it refuses to recognise the social process which is the generator of consciousness, emotion, thought, and of all products into which emotion and thought enter. Because ideology is rooted in the labour process, the decay of an economy must re-appear as a similar disintegration in the art or science which is rooted in it. Bourgeois economic contradictions are bourgeois ideological contradictions. The scientist and artist are forced on by the tension between past and present, tradition and experience. But tradition is the accumulated product of the past labour process as preserved; and experience is an experience in contemporary society.

Such a disintegration can only be revitalised by a transformation of the relations which, at the very roots, are destroying the creative forces of society. Change is dialectic; one quality gives birth to another by the revelation of the contradictions it contains, whose very tension begets the synthesis. The contradiction at the heart of bourgeois culture is becoming naked, and more and more clearly there is revealed the inextinguishable antagonism between the two classes of bourgeois economy, the bourgeoisie and the proletariat. The ruling class, the bourgeoisie, which exploits the labour power of the proletariat for profit, in doing so generates an illusion which sets the pattern for all the structure and ideology of bourgeois civilisation. Man is held to be free in proportion to his ignorance of the social process, as a part of which he functions. Instead of bourgeois activity being governed by knowledge of the social process, it is governed by the market, by the 'laws of supply and demand', by the free circulation of cash, in short, by mere 'accident', for accident is man's name for his ignorance of determinism. Man is held to be free by virtue of unrestricted rights over property: but this merely conceals the domination of a few, who own the means of production and can traffick in labour-power, over the many who have nothing but labour-power to sell. The few believe that this dominating power they exercise makes them free, that in the act of domination their actions are not determined; but the event—the internal collapse of their economy in war and crisis and of their ideology in anarchy—reveals that not even they the lords are free, but their desires have disrupted their culture.

And who can transform it? Only those who are conscious of the cause of its collapse, who realise that to be without conscious social organisation is not to be free, and that power over men by men is not freedom, even though concealed, but all the more if concealed, is mere ignorance of the necessities of society. It is precisely the proletarians who know all this by the pressure of the economy whose cruel weight they support. In their struggles against exploitation they learn that only conscious organisation, Trade Unions and factory Acts, can give them freedom from oppression. When they see their masters, the bourgeoisie, powerless to prevent war, unemployment, and the decay of the economy they have built up, the proletariat learns that this power of men over men, exercised by a simple act of the will and congealed in a property right, is not freedom for either class. It is only a delusive short cut in which humanity was for a time lost. Freedom appears, socially, when men take no short cuts of 'will' but learn the necessities of their own nature and of external reality and thus share a goal in common. Then the common goal and the nature of reality uniquely determine the only possible action without compulsion, as when two men combine, without 'orders', to lift a stone that lies in their path. In such an understanding, a new science, a new art, and a new society are already explicit, and to build it involves a proletariat which has already overthrown the bourgeoisie, and in revolution and reconstruction has transformed civilisation. In a society which is based on co-operation not on compulsion, and which is conscious, not ignorant of, necessity, desires as well as cognitions can be socially manipulated as part of the social process. Beauty will then return again, to enter consciously into every part of the social process. It is not a dream that labour will no longer be ugly, and the products of labour once again beautiful.

III

MEN AND NATURE

A Study in Bourgeois History

IN the course of our examination of bourgeois culture, we have always reached, at a certain stage in our analysis, a basic world-view which is the product of the bourgeois economy and gives a characteristic shape to every form of its ideology. It is not an error in the sense that it can be isolated, as a separate mistake, from every department of culture. It is only revealed on analysis as an unseen force, not explicit in the formulations of that culture but acting like a pressure from outside. It gives to that culture a characteristic distortion which is not visible to those who still live within the framework of that economy. This bourgeois world-view is not however a fixed consciousness. Like the society of which it is a product, it changes, and may even appear as its own opposite—just as a photograph has positive and negative components, and yet remains the same partial view of reality.

This world-view is the product of a society divided into classes, as all previous highly cultivated civilisations have been. The essence of all class-societies is that the ruling power is exercised by a minority. Social process is directed not by the necessities of the process alone—of which society is as yet not fully conscious—but by the wills of the ruling individuals. Thus the individual will appears as alone active and creative. The aim of all society—man's attempt to become free of the forces of nature—seems in such societies to be realised by passive obedience by the ruled to the will of the ruler, who is guided by his individual desires. This is how it appears to rulers and ruled. but in fact both classes are the outcome of a division of labour and derive their roles, not from Will but from their status in social production.

Such a division of the labour process, which involves a class passively and blindly labouring and another class directing these labours according to their consciousness of the necessities of the case, is both an advance and a weakness as compared with the primitive communism of the simplest societies, in which each member labours for the tribe without important distinction or difference. It is an advance because it involves a sharpening of consciousness at the pole of the ruling class and a more intensive production of social wealth. It is a weakness because it produces a deadening of consciousness at the pole of the ruled class and a cleavage between the conscious enjoyment of the ruling class and the blind action of the ruled class. It makes possible a permanent inequality of status because the ruling class, by virtue of directing the labour of the exploited, can also ensure the flow of the bulk of its products into their own lives, leaving to the exploited the minimum necessary to ensure an efficient existence.

Thus a material inequality is reflected in an inequality of consciousness. Not only does thinking become the prerogative of the exploiting class, but it also gradually becomes separated from action and moreover is favoured socially to the extent to which it separates itself from action, because it is just this separation which has generated its superior status as the mark of the ruling, 'cunning', or administrative class. This separation is anti-social because it hamstrings thought and baffles action; and yet it is produced by social forces.

The direction of their labours by the ruling class is not of course the result of a free election by the ruled in favour of the members of the ruling class. Were this the case they would not be a ruling class but organs of society, like the look-out animal posted by a herd of herbivores. Actually, their direction is coercive, and is enforced by the forms of society. The class is created by a *right*, a legal *form* of property, which is enforced by the conscious organs of society against the exploited class. This cannot be a right to an empty thing, but must be a property right in the *means of production*. In all societies the means of production have to be worked by men. In primitive societies virtually the only means of production are men and land, there is nothing else of economic importance, and here the right which forms the basis of a ruling class is the right to own land and men. In later civilisations it is also the right to own individually all those means of production without which men cannot exist. The right to own these, coercively enforced by society, ensures that the owning class rules the non-owning class, even without the right to own men.

The form of its ownership is what constitutes a class, and the rights of the ruling class, visible in its laws, conventions and religion, are also the expression of the main characteristics of the economy. The labour process is common to all societies; the division into exploiters and exploited is a feature peculiar to class societies; the form this division takes is peculiar to each particular class society. Slave-owning societies are divided, broadly, into free men and slaves; feudal societies into lords and serfs; developed bourgeois societies into capitalists and 'free' workers, who must bring their labour-power to market because they are excluded from ownership of all means of production.

The ideology of all such civilisations is that of the ruling class, for the division of labour into a class, functionally, of thinkers and a class, functionally, of labourers causes the aggregation of all social consciousness at the pole of the ruling class, as long as the division persists. Hence even the most developed culture expresses at its height the view of the ruling class—its aspirations, its vicissitudes, and its weaknesses. In a revolution, when power passes from one class to another, a corresponding ideological revolution takes place, though evidently this can only happen if the conditions of the labour process have developed an antagonistic consciousness in the exploited class.

Thinking emerges historically as a partner to action, both vested in the one individual. Their separation in the class division of society begets eventually a corresponding inefficiency of action and decay in thought, so that the collapse of a culture is marked simultaneously by a material decline and an ideological bankruptcy.

The division of labour is a progressive element in social development, and the fact that individuals genetically gifted with 'brains' perform directive rôles and others gifted for action perform active rôles is not in itself anything but desirable. Both thinker and actor then form part of the one social process, and there is a unity in social action as when an architect plans, a foreman directs, and labourers build a house. But the consciousness of a class society does not emerge as the consciousness of a specific labour process, for then there would not be a class ruling on the basis of property right, but administrators or administrative organs, thrown up by society according to the necessities of the labour process. But this consciousness emerges divorced from action or from society, as a right inherent in the individual or in the nature of things. If this right emerged from the necessities of the social process it would not need formal protection; it does not so emerge and must therefore be secured and protected by laws, by the visible forms of society, which must therefore be *class* forms. The right may come by inheritance, by being born or called to a status which carries with it the right or by some kind of formal transfer between individuals. And all the forms of society are directed to defending the right.

Hence we do not in such societies get men naturally and by the consent of society emerging as thinkers, but consciousness is established as the right of a class, which at the best can only be painfully won by a few in other classes, who are then sucked into the ruling class. It is this buttressing of rights which produces the characteristic distortion in the ideology of that class, and this class ideology is, as we have seen, also the ideology of that society's whole culture. All such ideologies of a ruling class have this in common, that they see thought, consciousness, will, (their class prerogatives) not as determined by action or by the outer reality which thought goes out in action to know and change, but as innate—free in the sense in which they regard themselves as free. Consciousness becomes a privilege which is not actively created but which is 'given' by birth or chance. This is an illusion, and cannot be pursued without revealing its contradictions. It is the illusion common to all class-cultures, and therefore to all the ideologies so far produced by history except that of dialectical materialism.

In bourgeois society the distorting effect of the illusion is least in physics, which is consequently the first science to emerge in that society and the last to collapse. The distortion will necessarily be greatest in the sphere of social relations, in the science of society or *history*, and in fact of bourgeois history one can ask—has bourgeois history yet been born? History as interpreted by bourgeois culture has shown only the faintest resemblance to a scientific discipline, and this applies most sharply to those very historians who regard themselves as truly scientific and objective.

Indeed, the creation of a science of history involves the doom of bourgeois culture. It is for this reason that bourgeois historians have so frequently arrived at the conclusion that history is not, and cannot be, a science. They were correct in this measure, that history cannot be a science within the sphere of bourgeois culture.

Capitalist economy, as it develops its contradictions, reveals, as at opposed poles, on the one hand the organisation of labour in the factory, in the trust, in the monopoly; on the other hand the disorganisation of labour in the competition between these units. The development of monopoly and the increase of amalgamations by no means eases the tension of the transition to a completely organised world of industry. Such a transition requires the extinction of capitalist property and the end of the exploitation of labour, but the increasing organisation *within* the monopoly produces increasing competition *between* the monopolies. The amalgamations of capitalist economy result in violent and disruptive struggles on the part of profit-seeking capital to find elbow room for profit outside 'stabilised' markets. 'Stabilisasion' thus generates acute instability, and the nationalisation of a market by a monopoly produces a flow of profit which, just because the market is self-limited by monopoly, cannot be used in it and is therefore exported to weaker markets as a new disruptive factor. This external disorganisation, which is intensified by increasing internal organisation as long as it takes place within the categories of bourgeois economy, is seen clearly to-day in the growth of economic nationalism and Fascism, and the fresh round of imperialist wars now preparing.

But just the same phenomenon is seen in bourgeois ideology. We have highly organised sciences or departments of biology, physics, psychology, anthropology, engineering, æsthetics, education, economics, philology, and the like, and yet not only do they not form an integrated world-view, but their very increase of internal organisation produces a disorganisation of culture as a whole. As the result of the development of its constituent disciplines, bourgeois culture is violently disrupted—the same disaster as is befalling capitalist economy, and due ultimately to the same cause.

The only real solution of the contradictions of capitalist economy is of course the elimination of the factor which produces the external disorganisation in spite of the internal organisation. As soon as the external disorganisation grows faster than the internal organisation (which has been the case since 1900), from that time bourgeois economy is doomed, and only awaits the hand of whatever executioner history has provided—in this case the proletariat. This doom involves the complete socialisation of production and the realisation by society of the laws of its own functioning, through consciousness of which it becomes able to organise itself.

Capitalist economy has become conscious of the environment. It knows the necessities involved in making matter obey its will. It has done so with the illusion that this control alone is sufficient to force nature to obey man's will. But the knowledge of non-human necessities is not enough to ensure the conquest of nature. Man is a part of nature, and it is not man in the abstract of which society is composed but of actual men, in given times and places. The conquest of nature is the work of these men organised in a society, and nature only obeys 'man' in so far as this organisation, or 'civilisation' is an accomplished fact, and she by no means obeys 'a man', an *individual*, except in so far as his purpose is a part of the purpose of organised men as a whole. This involves co-operation. A number of individuals striving for antagonistic ends is itself disorganisation and will result, not in nature obeying one man's will (for the others negate it) or the sum of wills (for the wills contradict each other), but in a mean which will reflect none of their wills—such an unwished-for result as a war or a slump.

A man does not control nature by knowing the laws necessary to make hats, or by being free of the domain of physics, for nature obeys not man the individual but men organised in a society, and fulfils not any particular will but the historic outcome of all wills in action. Therefore men must know in addition to the necessities of 'nature', the necessities of co-operation, and the historic outcome of actions undertaken socially. This knowledge is part and parcel of the co-operation of social action, for if it is known that such and such actions are necessary to attain an end, those actions must be taken. Hence such a knowledge involves the overthrow of bourgeois economy and its replacement by communist economy.

But bourgeois economy is not homogeneous—it is a class society. Indeed that very class division is what produces its characteristic form. There is always a class to whose individual wills all society bends and whose individual wills are in the sum realised in the conquest of nature, whatever the consequences to the rest of society. This class of victorious wills, the ruling class, is one that, as capitalist economy decays, necessarily grows more limited. The area of freedom in capitalist economy progressively contracts. But this by no means involves the peaceful vacation by this class of their thrones, for their possession of all social freedom, while it is a diminishing freedom in sum, is also one which, because the class itself is attenuated, is *per capita* greater. Thus the inducement to struggle to retain their power increases at the same rate as their power as individuals over social production increases. But at the other pole, the forces of the unfree gather.

All this is reflected in the present state of culture. Witnessing its widespread disorganisation, we ask: 'How can men's knowledge of the necessities of 'nature', as evidenced in biology, physics and the rest, be integrated and reconciled in a connected world-view, and made useful to man so that it becomes more than theoretical knowledge—knowledge active in society?

The answer is: 'Only by an understanding of the crucible in which this knowledge was generated'. Is this not the function of psychology? No, for psychology is the science of the individual mind and all its various forms of consciousness. These forms themselves are given it by its experiences, and these are social experiences. The disorganisation of these internally organised but closed worlds of human knowledge can only be cured by an understanding of the very thing of which they are the product—of society. It is not man, the individual, who produces science; the criterion of a scientific truth is that it is *objective*, that it can be tested by other men—not by all men (lunatics and morons and savants) but men as socially organised, and hence, through the actions and appropriate organisation of society, competent to test these truths. The 'solution' of the anarchy of bourgeois culture is the same as for bourgeois economy, that men become conscious of the necessities of themselves, not as individuals or as humanity in the undifferentiated abstract, but as men in social action—in the case of economy as a whole, this means conscious as men actually engaged in producing for social ends; and in the case of ideology in particular it means conscious as men actually engaged in studying reality for social ends. But men—real, contemporary individuals—can only become so conscious as they are part of the transformation of bourgeois into communist culture, as real participants in the mêlée of the revolutionary struggle, which transformation is itself the result of the actions of the anti-bourgeois class, the proletariat. The proletariat, because of its position and organisation in bourgeois society, is the vanguard of the fight. It seems therefore that to understand history it is necessary to make it, and this in fact is the case; it is a necessity in which history is not different from but similar to other sciences.

The ground plan of history as a science was laid by Marx and Engels, and was an outcome of their own participation in the history-making struggle of the working-class at that time—the first stage in the anti-bourgeois offensive of the proletariat. This science of Marx and Engels is *historical materialism*—a view of the world as a unity because it is a material world, and a view of the world as a development because it has a history. When bourgeois culture has been completely replaced by communist culture, as the result of a social revolution and its aftermath of socialist construction, then all the organised disciplines of bourgeois culture will be integrated in a consistent world-view. That world-view will necessarily be historical—that is to say, it will be the view of the development of men as socially organised beings, not an arbitrary or spontaneous development, but a determined process. Psychology, biology, and physics will not be *absorbed* by history, any more than factory organisation or school organisation or theatre organisation will be absorbed by social organisation. By the removal of the disruptive factor, private profit, these organisations will generate the social organisation and, as a result of this organisation, themselves differentiate and become enriched. The renaissance of history will not therefore be the amalgamation of the sciences, but the removal of the hidden force that was distorting and isolating them to an increasing degree. Once this is removed, they will communicate, and this communication will be history. This communication will revitalise them and raise them to new heights, for it is just their isolation and their ignorance of their own roots in social process that is holding back their development.

If man has, so far, been unable to write history, it means that all civilisation up to the present has been a part of the prehistoric stage of society. Man's understanding of history in a scientific sense is shown by his capacity to make it, not blindly but according to his will; just as his understanding of physics is shown by his ability to make the elements fulfil his predictions. Thus the understanding of history is involved with that very transition from the realm of necessity to the realm of freedom which is the characteristic of the last stage of pre-history, the emergence of the proletariat as a class to end classes and so inaugurate an *historic* civilisation.

Marx was the first who was able to show that history was really made by men—not by man in the abstract as a developing animal, nor by outstanding men as sporadic forces, but constantly by the whole group of individuals existing in society. That is not to say he saw history as the story of a group, for this is again to abstract, to lump concrete individuals into an ideal group. It was because history was the story of different individuals playing different parts that the relations between them were important, and just because they arose as the result of society's action on matter, their expression in art, morals, science, religion and law were real factors in the history of society. It was because Marx saw that history was the story of all individuals that he saw it must be the science of *organised* society, for only in organisation do individuals acquire a meaning; it is only by virtue of the warp and woof of manifold relations engendered by social relations, which intersect in nodes, that the nodes or individuals are individualised and become more than specimens of a species.

What is history? It is the story of men. But men may be considered as lumps of matter, and as such they perform in the course of time certain movements. This is not the subject of history, but of physics. History is interested in those qualitative innovations of mankind which differentiate it from 'nature'—from dead matter and animals. History is the law of motion of men, not as matter or as living breathing organisms or as animals, but as something distinct from all these spheres, as *socially organised* animals.

History then only begins where physics, physiology and biology leave off. The laws of physics pervade all spheres, but physiology and biology have also new laws. The laws of physiology in turn are valid in biology which, however, is the domain of qualitatively new laws. History only starts when fresh laws, inclusive of but additional to physical, physiological and biological laws begin to operate, and the evolution and change of these laws is the subject of history. It is only in this sphere that we can begin to speak of history. But what is it that distinguishes man, in all stages of humanity, from the beasts? Marx had only to ask and answer this question, to uncover the whole sphere of laws appropriate to history.

History has this peculiarity additional to other sciences that, as it were, it forces man to bend round and look himself in the eyes.

Having proceeded through physics, physiology and biology to history, he finds as part of history, the production of these very sciences, which it thus transcends. The ideological circle is then closed, but only when it has included as material factors, as things linked together causally at each stage, every sphere of human activity. And the closure is only spatial—for history is what men make and men continue to live, and history, and all the ideologies of whose genesis it is the record, continue to unfold. It unfolds in the present, in our action as we live and move in the real society of to-day. Closed ideologically, the circle is open in action with which it is therefore unified. History leads from and through action to man's mind.

But the last thing the bourgeois wishes to do is to look himself in the eyes.

Marx's answer to the question, What is it that differentiates man from the animals? is this, that man is organised and organised in a social way: there is no such thing as lone man, but only real living men, and not merely men clumped like swarming locusts, but arranged in social relations arising out of economic production. The co-operation necessary to production makes them unite, and makes them men.

But (it may be said) the bees, ants and wasps unite for economic production, and this does not make them human. True, and what is the biological difference between the social insects and man? With them, this organisation is instinctive: bees and wasps in any situation will reproduce it. But men will not reproduce their society instinctively. European culture and capitalism are not instinctive. Men, turned as babes into a jungle, would wander through it as mere brutes, without individuality or consciousness, feral and dumb.

This proves that man's behaviour, ideas, art, science, laws, ethics, technique are not in *him*, in his genetic make-up. In his genetic make-up is only plasticity, the potentiality of this or a thousand other shapes. These things must therefore all be outside him and imprinted on him, not as a stereotype prints a drawing, mechanically, but rather as a body cell, by being in a certain part of the embryo and in a certain relation to other parts, becomes a bone, fat, or epidermal cell, and yet if transplanted will change its nature according to its new situation.

What is there then, outside man the unit, which has this effect on him? Simply the relations into which he enters with other men, not willingly but because he is born into such a society, just as its relations with other cells affect the body cell, not voluntarily but because it is in such a place. Thus all the social relations expressed in all the possible interactions between man and man become, with Marx's interpretation, not something superadded to humanity or 'put into practice' by man, but something which makes the concrete man what he is. But, being so made, he makes other men different, still through these same real channels. Thus there is a real meaning to the definition of man as organised men, which separates it from the apparent organisation of the hive. The organisation is more than the individual men and cannot be predicted from the bare babe, because it has a law of growth of its own, occupying æons; but still it is an organisation of *men.* It is not an environment. The organisation of, for example, moths swarming round a flame or beasts round a salt lick is *environmental*; the organisation of bees in a hive is *innate.* But the organisation of men, which produces the very phenomena which history is to study, is neither; it is *social.*

History thus becomes, not the study of individuals, of their innate capacities and responsive changes to stimuli (for that is psychology) nor the study of the influence of the environment on men (for that is ecology) but it is the study of this organisation which is neither innate nor given in the environment, and which although it is the organisation of men in nature has a law of development neither human nor natural but economic. Now it is certain that bourgeois culture could not analyse this organisation, for it is just this organisation which bourgeois economy, as its pre-requisite, denies and veils in every possible way. Bourgeois culture is constantly proclaiming man the individual against this organisation, and is continually involving itself in contradiction, for all the qualities it calls 'individual', so far from being antagonistic to organisation are generated by it, and the very state which it claims to be produced by organisation—featureless, unfree man—is man as he exists if robbed of organisation, or as he must have been before he passed from brute to human. This also involves that the bourgeois, struggling for these precious individualities, produces to his consternation still higher degrees of organisation, and struggling against organisation, produces a loss of individuality. Because he is struggling blindly he produces everything unexpectedly and anarchically, and he shows his lack of history by this simple test, that he is unable to make history consciously. History must always be made because men, conscious or unconscious, still live and so history comes into being for the bourgeois as a series of surprises and catastrophes—the opposite to what he desires. Man still remains, although the subject of history, in the prehistoric stage of culture.

But why, asks Marx, does this organisation come into being at all? It is not just *any* organisation—a chance arrangement of men, for it is evident that it has an evolution: that is to say, each stage is caused by and is born from the preceding stage. Why, if it is not determined by an instinct, is it not determined by the environment, and if it is not determined by either, is not its cause outside the Universe, undetermined, immaterial, and unknowable ? If one could explain how this organisation came into being, one could grasp its internal law of motion, and then the movement of history would be understood and man could make history consciously.

Either this organisation is divine, immaterial and unknowable, or it must come from the one activity which would form part of the Universe, and yet be distinguishable from man and environment taken separately—it must come from the interaction of men and environment *together*. If these are separate, and then come together and produce a transaction, this transaction is a new and yet a determined material entity, and the result or synthesis is the starting point for a fresh movement.

But what is the interaction of man and environment, by which both are changed—both instinctual man and natural environment? This interaction is economic production, and it is true that it is just this which distinguishes man, at the earliest levels we know, from the animals. The visible results of this interaction, the real factors in history, are *environmentalised* men and *humanised* environment.

What is meant by environmentalised men? How can a human being be said to be conditioned by the environment?

In this way. If, for example, men wish to act upon the environment—say, to move a log—the shape of the log requires that a certain minumum number unite, that they all push together, and that they arrange themselves round the log in certain ways. They have then been organised by the task—by the necessities of the piece of nature to which they found themselves opposed.

They have also themselves changed as a result. Participation in the task has added to their knowledge of logs. They may as a result of many such different tasks come to invent the lever, and now in levering the log, they will be organised by the task in a different way. One level of organisation has led to another.

Thus all the distinctive qualities of man—his consciousness of reality, as for example the detachability of logs (science), his emotional relations as when all push heartily together on the log (art), his social relations as when one instructs others when to push (law, ethics, convention), his medium for socially integrating experience and volitions in connection with the log (language, writing), are environmental. So, it is true, are the organic adaptations to the water of the otter or the whale.

But whereas such organic adaptations are adaptations of the individual to the environment, those of men are *adaptations of the social relations of a body of men* to the environment. The otter is adapted to the water through his innate corporeal transformations. Man is still better adapted to the water, but only through society, because society has built ships, created ports, developed navigation, and can so master the water. Man's adaptations are not to the water, but to society, which only as a *whole*, as an organised co-operative system, is adapted to the water. Man's speech, physical knowledge and civic pride are not directly adapted to the water; they are adapted to an organised society, and only in organised society is there a human adaptation to water. When we say environmentalised man, we mean therefore men with an organisation produced among them by the necessities of the environment, and not men with individual changes like the otter's flat tail, produced in them by the environment. But since men are organised and are the units of the organisation, they are changed by it. They are not as units changed (like the otter) by the environment; they are changed as units by the organisation in which they participate to face the environment. They do not, as bare men and units, face the environment: as such units they face only organised society, into which they are born. What is this organisation? It is the organisation into which men are forced when as a body they work together to change the environment. It is the organisation imposed by economic production which generates the non-instinctive and characteristically human qualities.

The same organisation is also reflected in the humanised environment. The environment too is changed, not merely by the movement of material (cities, roads, port, ships, machinery, cultivated plants, agriculture, clearings), but also because this very process, by revealing the structure of reality more clearly, makes the environment different *for* man. The cosmos of our culture is a different environment from the cosmos of Egyptian man; and equally men, by being changed, become different for the environment and different for each other. The man of modern psychology and physiology is not the man of the Australian corroboree; the cosmos-for-the-blackfellow is not the cosmos-for-us.

Thus what we call organisation is the outcome of one double process—the environmentalisation of organised men, begetting all the human values—language, science, art, religion, consciousness; and the humanisation of nature, begetting the material changes in nature and man's own greater understanding of reality. Thus the development of humanity is not the increasing separation of man from a 'state of nature'. It is man's increasing interpenetration with nature. History is not, as the bourgeois supposes, the story of man in himself, or of human 'nature' (which changes too little to be the subject of history) but the story of this increasing interpenetration of nature by man as a result of his struggle with it. It is the story of economic production. The story of man is not the story of the increasing subjection of man's freedom and individuality to organisation in order to cope with nature, but his growth of freedom and individuality through organisation imposed by nature, in his interaction with it. The impossibility of ever finding human values or material causes separate in history is due to this very fact, that history is the study of their increasing interpenetration and of the rich development of this inseparable network of relations. History is the study of the object-subject relation of men-nature, and not of either separately. It is the study of the products of men acting on nature and being acted on by it. Nature never finds itself faced by individual men, but always by men working co-operatively in economic production; and man never finds himself faced by nature directly, but always by society organised by nature.

Thus, as a result of economic production a man finds himself born not into nature, but into a society already organised by interpenetration with nature, and into a nature already changed and X-rayed by this. He does not ever at any stage consciously form a society; society forms him. He in turn, as a result, is an active centre for a fresh transformation; he in turn forms society. Thus social development proceeds, and this is history.

History occurs not only on the human side, for, though society changes nature, nature so changed imposes fresh forms of organisation on society.

Which comes first then in time, the individual man or society? Did not individual men ever find themselves without society and, having regard to the necessities of the case, consciously enter into social co-operation? No, society came first, for it would have been sub-human anthropoids, unconsciously and blindly forced to enter into some rude forms of economic production unknown to other animals, which were by this very activity forced to become men.

Versions of History

It was Marx who first laid bare then the subject of history, which was not till then distinguished and is to-day still not distinguished within the categories of bourgeois culture. He first showed that all men's activities are the subject of history and must be included in it. He showed that not merely 'great men' working along special channels, 'important ideas' or special occasions—'times of ferment'—produce the motion of civilisation; but every man, in the active relations he enters into with other men, has a causal rôle in determining the movements of history. Such a notion had before only been conceived under the false notion of a whole people passively and solidly providing the background of history, while great men, great occasions, and great cultures acted as accidental disturbances or inflammations of this passive lump. Marx's analysis of social relations was evolutionary and therefore revolutionary: it was from the activity of the people themselves, as a causal result, that great men, great occasions, and great cultures emerged, and in turn developed an internal law of motion.

Bourgeois culture, which set itself at its best period the task of understanding everything around it, has certainly *attempted* a causal scheme of history. It was doomed to fail in this attempt for the same reason as bourgeois philosophy was doomed to fail, because it seized hold first of the object as distinct from the subject, and then, forced by the logic of reality to seize the subject, it found itself in an equally untenable position. Subject and object, although opposite poles, interpenetrate. In the individual this interpenetration is sensation. In men this interpenetration is history. It is an *active* interpenetration, and in proportion as bourgeois culture becomes the culture of a class whose role is consciousness, and which is divorced from the exploited class whose task is action, there occurs the separating out of the two elements of sensation. Then both history and epistemology disintegrate.

The first causal scheme of history which bourgeois culture gave birth to was the environmental or metaphysical-materialist explanation, according to which man's social history is the result of his environment. A hot climate produces black races. Where there is coal, there will spring up an industrial culture. In the cold zones man is necessarily a hunter. On rivers and by the sea he is a navigator or fisher. Fertile zones support dense populations and make possible town life. Regular floods ensure the creation of a settled agriculture.

Now this explanation, in spite of its power, ultimately has fatal weaknesses. It ignores the active creative rôle of man, and envisages him as passively moulded by the environment; this obviously cannot be the case.

For example, coal exists in many parts of the world: but only in a certain place and in a certain time did it give rise to industrial predominance. In other places cultural development was built up on water power. There are thousands of islands in the world: on some the inhabitants have no boats; on others, craft ranging from coracles and bladders to ocean-going liners. The ancient Britons lived over coal-seams, but for them the coal did not exist, and could not therefore determine their existence.

This reveals the 'hole' in the mechanical-materialist interpretation. The conditioning resources of Nature only exist, as determinants, insofar as from being things-in-themselves they become things-for-us. Coal did not exist for the ancient Briton because he had no technique for extracting it. The technique depends on a certain social organisation, when the necessary division of labour (capitalist mining) exists to make coal a determining social factor. Similarly, air only exists as an important transport medium for a race which has the necessary technique and social organisation to fly, and water only exists as a means of navigation for races able to build boats, the size and complexity of their boats in turn depending on their state of economic development.

Thus any scheme which makes the material configuration of the environment the determining factor in civilisation fails because it does not see that the environment is not something fixed. As environment, its very qualities depend on the subject, man, and primarily on his social organisation. It becomes an environment mineable in places only when technique and social organisation make mining possible. It becomes an environment which can be tilled and will produce crops in places, only when social organisation has advanced to a stage where culture is possible. It becomes an environment which can be navigated in places only when social organisation makes possible the building and sailing of ships.

Thus, although the environment in the form of rivers, iron, coal and air contains determining factors for society at each stage of its evolution, which factors prove determinant depends upon the technical and social organisation of man at that stage: in brief, on his economic production. The environment as environment is changed by economic production, not merely in its reality but in its potentiality. Thus the causal role in history cannot be played by the environment as an active matrix for passive society, for society itself selects at each stage, not arbitrarily but as a result of precedent evolution, which are to be the determining factors in the environment.

On the realisation of this the explanation of history by environment breaks down, for after stripping from society all qualities not purely environmental, nothing recognisably human is left. It does not follow that the environment plays no part in determining history. On the contrary, at every stage the environment-for-man is determinant. But the environment-for-man changes at every stage, and its change must therefore be sought in society.

This leads to the idealistic interpretation of history, in which history is made by man's desires, ideas, and aims. But this theory is wrecked on the opposite difficulty to that of the mechanical-materialist explanation. The latter is unable to explain the change of the environment, the former is unable to explain the constancy of man—by constancy, we mean his constancy as bare individual. If a Melanesian, an ancient Athenian and a modern English babe were allowed to grow up in a wood, or for that matter a deserted town or factory, none would show any of the characteristics of its parents' culture— either their language, their economic production, or their consciousness. They would grow up sub-human. This shows that man remains through the ages relatively unchanged, or that at least his genetic change is in no way proportioned to his change as a member of contemporary society. This raises the dilemma, how can the unchanging genotype, acting on the environment, beget the change we have discussed? The answer can only be that it is a change, not in individual man but in his association—in that interpenetration of man with nature which is neither man alone nor bare nature, but is a system of economic production, including on the one hand machines, plant, capital and cities, and on the other hand the social relations, science, art, law and culture which have been generated by this system. This system, although it is composed of units and of environment, has a history and a law of motion to to be found in the analysis of the unit or the environment separately.

Thus it is that bare man, born into this system, becomes moulded by it and so changed in turn operates through the system on the environment and brings about further changes which are the basis of a new departure.

Ideas themselves can only be the product of such an existing organisation. Napoleon, Caesar or Plato gets his language, the things he sees, his assumptions and desires, from engaging in social life, from being educated and living in a Greek city or Rome or Republican France.

That is not to say that ideas are a mere iridescence. On the contrary, it is precisely in Marxism that ideas become real things, being both caused and in turn creating an effect. Darwin's consciousness, being formed, undergoes its own law of development and produces changes in the system in which he lives. Just as the environment, with indefinite potentialities-in-itself, reveals successively new, definite potentialities for man as a result of the evolution of technique, so bare man, with indefinite possibilities of consciousness, reveals a consciousness appropriate to the system in which he finds himself, either Melanesian or Athenian. Man's consciousness then is a real determining factor in history, but it is not man's consciousness that produces at each stage social organisation for economic production, but social organisation for economic production which produces man's consciousness. Being is prior to thinking, and we can easily see that this must be so, for all living organisms engage in activity which is not conscious activity, and this unconscious activity is phylogenetically and ontogenetically prior to conscious activity. Thus in the human body the sympathetic system acts unconsciously and is prior to and more fundamental than the more highly organised conscious activities. It is just because consciousness is subtle and richer, that it is sequent to unconsciousness.

No analysis of society which aims to be really causal can take consciousness as prior, and write history in terms of man's desires and ideas. True, history is made partly by the conscious actions of men, and any causal explanation must include consciousness; but it must include consciousness as it develops historically, as an outcome of the development of economic production and the division of labour.

And although men's history-making actions are conscious and willed, the results by no means tally with the aims, but are in fact often quite other. Indeed this is the chief characteristic of the prehistoric stage of civilisation. How then can ideas play a causal role, in the sense that history is their realisation, when events contradict men's intentions? Only if, opposing the intentions, there is a kind of devil or evil force, and this ceases to be a causal explanation. If we take as primary the interpenetration of man with nature, of which ideas are the most refined product, we are then in a position to explain both the disasters and the successes of ideas, and to understand why men will and act as they do, and why their volition and actions produce the results we know. Living precedes ideas; and men must breathe and be fed to have them.

Because of the failure of the theory of consciousness as the causal explanation of history, an attempt was made by later idealists to make the cause of history, not ideas in the heads of men (conscious purposes) but ideas absolute and out of the heads of men. Certainly these absolute ideas outside the heads of men need no sustenance nor determining cause, but just because of that they furnish no causal explanation of history. Of these explanations by absolute ideas (fixed 'cycles of decay'; realisations of 'Hellenic and Faustian cultures') the best known and most consistent is Hegel's. Such an explanation is faced with the dilemma of admitting, either that these absolute ideas now exist really and that therefore evolution is at an end, or do not really exist, in which case causation is explained as the work of non-existents, and this is easily seen for the logical trick it is. Again, if these absolute ideas are real existents now, either in the past the absolute ideas existed or were later generated by the process of history. If the former, then how can reality and the ideas be in mutually-determining relation; if the latter, how can the ideas be the cause of that which has generated them?

In Spengler's crude form, or in the absurd form given it by Fisher (who explains bourgeois civilisation as the evolution of 'the ideal of liberty') absolute idealism shows itself even less adequate than with Hegel, and, as compared with mechanical-materialism, is a mark of the increasing poverty of bourgeois thought.

Obviously the environmental 'explanation' of history corresponds to mechanical-materialism in bourgeois philosophy, with neo-Darwinism in biology, and with behaviourism in psychology. Similarly the purposive 'explanation' corresponds to idealism in philosophy, neo-Lamarckianism in biology, and the instinct and hormic schools in psychology.

As these explanations by their own development expose their bankruptcy, there is regression to a kind of history which is believed to be a compromise, or synthesis, but which is in fact nothing but a confession of the breakdown of the culture producing it. This sytem has as its expression in philosophy, positivism or phenomenalism, but it is constantly being forced by its own contradictions into a confused eclecticism. How does this positivism appear in bourgeois history?

Positivism asserts that man's sole concern is with sensa, or phenomena. Since subject and object are, according to positivism, alike inaccessible (for the object is an unknowable thing-in-itself) sensa are the sole data of science and no true statements as to reality are possible. Laws are merely convenient summaries or lucky predictive accidents. Since the object is declared unknowable, the real ground of causality—the material basis of sensation—is eliminated. The world no longer possesses a unity due to its materiality, and sensa are connected in no causal way: anything *might* happen.

Of course such an attitude is a negation of science and in its pure form is hardly practicable. The subject or the object is in fact smuggled in illegitimately by some backdoor. For example, laws become convenient statements (Mach), or the world becomes the work of a mathematician (Jeans). In this way a spurious unity is given to some restricted field of reality. A collection of such spurious unities not themselves unified, a farrago of mutually contradictory categories, becomes the content of science when any large domain of reality is surveyed. Thus positivism necessarily involves eclecticism.

This is visible in bourgeois history in two forms. First of all there is the monstrously detailed collection of facts, of inscriptions, pipe rolls, potsherds, and records of every description which become valued simply for their own sake, as if a sufficient accumulation of them would eventually in some mysterious way give birth to a history. This would be a correct assumption if such detail work were part of an ordered programme, had a method, or were carried out at the impulse of a general science of history with understood laws and a causal programme. Instead, it is like a curiosity shop; it is the collecting of detail for its own sake, and since the domain of history is all men's activities, the jackdaw accumulation of such facts can proceed indefinitely until not all the volumes of mankind could hold the records. No science of history, however, would have been produced even then, for it is the function of science to control and direct the collection of such facts now and, in this control and direction, to receive confirmation, negation or transformation. Such an accumulation, as long as it remains fundamentally unscientific, only adds to the confusion.

Men's opinions of events, however resurrected and authentic, do not form history, for we do not learn the characteristics of an epoch by learning the opinions of its members concerning it, any more than we learn the character of a man by his opinion of himself. We do not learn the laws of history's movement from the intentions of its units, for events, though produced by the conscious actions of men, do not realise their hopes. We learn these laws, as we learn those of the physiology of bodies and the evolution of animals, by the objective study of what exists independent of consciousness, in the course of a development in which theory marches step by step with practice, and the observed fact at every stage must transform the theory. If no general theory applying to all men's activities exists, how can even the most minute study of the records of dead men's activities be of value?

History is an evolution, a change; and we can no more expect to derive the real pressure and being of a civilisation from its language and material surroundings at any stage than we could expect naked man, put into a deserted London, to become a modern Londoner. All social qualities derive from society in movement, inheriting capital and transforming it, and we cannot understand the congealed products of each stage—its records—without understanding the metabolism of the society that produced them. We might as soon attempt to recreate the appearance and habit of the fossil animal from his bones without a study of living organisms to-day.

The staggering accumulation of unrelated petty detail which is bourgeois history to-day, naturally produces attempts at organisation. These contradict the basic positivism of the approach, and have to be smuggled in illegitimately. These attempts are necessarily restricted to limited fields: one historian will explain Egyptian history as the product of Nilotic conditions; another will explain the decline of Greece in terms of malaria; a third will explain bourgeois history as the growth of the idea of liberty, a fourth will explain medieval history as the triumph of Christo-Roman conceptions of order; a fifth will explain the development of the human race as a result of mineral deficiency; a sixth will explain the diffusion of heliolithic culture by the attraction of gold deposits; a seventh will explain the growth of capitalist economy by the bringing back of bullion from

South America, and so on, endlessly. Faced with the task of explaining the whole domain of culture, the historian has no hesitation in combining Freudian, behaviouristic, diffusionistic, pathological, idealistic and materialistic explanations, even though their premises are mutually contradictory. How can such a mixture call itself history, if by history is understood any causal or scientific account of men's activities in Time?

But history, as a science, is history in the present. It is science separating the past as preserved in the present. No one can cognise the past directly. But this separation of the past from the present is in fact the function of all sciences, for in so far as the universe has a history, all sciences have as their task the understanding of how things come into being and are at each stage determined by their past. Thus, just as the foundation of biology is evolution and metabolism, so the foundation of physics is cosmogony and motion. Yet this study of the past of the domain of qualities proper to the science in question has one main end, that of discovering the law of motion of all qualities comprised in it, their passage from not-being into being and back again.

This law of motion is discovered with a purpose; for just as the discovery through cosmogony of the most universal laws of physics, and, through paleontology, of the most universal laws of life, taught men the structure of physics-now and life-now, so the discovery through history of the most universal laws of society, teaches men the structure of society-now. But it does not rest there. There is passage not only to the past from the present but back again. Thus our knowledge of physiology and embryology is derived from paleontology, but then, equipped with knowledge derived from physiology, we turn with fresh understanding to those relics of the past which were the starting point of our researches. It is not a mere dialectic movement of *theory*.

The theory develops because at each stage it issues in active experiment and prediction: biology develops in experiments with organisms, in predictions of where and for what to look among fossils or evolutionary survivals; biology grows. Physics develops in experiments with bridges and engines, in predictions of what to look for in the field of space. Thus a science is always this separation out from the present of the past which, having being conserved in the present is different, and begets a dialectic antagonism which generates the future. This is merely the reflection in theory of what happens in reality, where the past is also preserved, by the conservation laws in the present, and by a kind of polar tension produces the new.

But the two processes, the theoretical and the objective, do not run on 'in parallel'. They intermingle, for the theoretical is the reflex of the objective and at every stage is seen to be the result of a material movement. Theory is always transformed as the result of a practical, objective transaction. History therefore appears as the most vital of the sciences in this respect, that it is the study of the very movement of society which generates the other sciences and itself.

Thus history too cannot escape from the method and life of all other sciences, which is to separate the past from the present in the only way in which it can be separated, as a contradiction, as a negation, which is synthesised in the future. The past to history is all that is-not-here, all that is not-in-the-present, and yet we in the present are studying it now in the present; but because, hitherto unconscious of this past, we now become conscious of it, we are not what we were, we are changed, something new has come to be. The present is now something new; it is the future. All this is not theoretical; it takes place both in action and thought. That is what we mean when we say, 'The separation, as a negation, of the past from the present, begets the *negation of the negation*, the "past as seen by the present", which is the future'.

The process is not contemplative, it is active. The change can only be a real change if new consciousness is not a mere iridescence, but a real entity, determining and determined. In fact consciousness, in its full active realisation, is just such a real determining entity. New consciousness (new knowledge, theory, or hypothesis) can only come into being as the result of an action, an experiment, a contact with reality which negates existing consciousness and as the result of this tension produces new consciousness—a new theory, hypothesis, or system of knowledge. This is the method of individual sensation, but when dealing with categories of sensation socially valid and generally organised, it becomes the method of science.

It must equally be the method of history. History cannot seize hold of the past by a divine ingestion; it can only seize hold of the present in the past. It cannot extract a theory from the present by an undetermined, one-way contemplation; it can only do so by testing at each stage its historical theories in practice. Its historical theories are precisely its conscious formulations of man's destiny, purpose, and rôle. History is an analysis of all the statements about man that are made in his laws, his ethics, his art, his religion, his science, and his hopes, and it puts this analysis into practice by living according to them or alternatively by denying them and transforming them. Hence the science of history is part of the practical activity of living according to the social consciousness of an age or alternatively of rebelling against it and transforming it. Indeed this must be so, for if history deals with all man's activities—his hates, loves and hopes as well as his building and feeding—it cannot be separated from his loving, hating, building and feeding now: if history is the theory of how he did these in the past, it cannot neglect the theory of how he does these in the present, and since science at every stage passes over into practice, it cannot neglect to undertake the confirmation or transformation of these activities now.

*   *   *   *   *

This is not merely the method of sensation and science, it is the general method of man's living. Thus, when men begin to question in any age the contemporary theory of social relations embodied in their art, their science, their laws, their morality, their system of social distribution, status, and rights, then it is a sign that their practical experience has proved the defects, or 'errors', in the ideological system as a whole or in part; but it is also a sign that, given in the very facts of their experience which expose the falsity of this superstructure, is the outline of the new superstructure which will more adequately express their real concrete being. The transformation accomplished, being and thinking are both on a new level, are both transformed by the interaction and ready for a new development.

This then explains the *evolution* of society. The primary factor is concrete being: the actual production in which men engage more or less consciously and willingly but which, considered as a whole, is unconscious. This is the evolution of technique—associated men changing nature as step by step the necessities of nature progressively unfold in reciprocal contact with technique, so that each reflects the other and yet both change for each other. This is the massive basis of society, and just as man may only eat, or eat and think, but cannot only think, so this developing technique with all the division of labour and the sharpening differentiation and increasing complexity it produces, is not all conscious and in any case is never conscious in one head, but is accompanied on the one hand by plexi of unrelated desires, hopes and thoughts in individual heads which are born and die, and, on the other hand by shared desires, hopes and thoughts which endure in the form of language, scientific disciplines, art products, traditions, conventions, laws and moralities. The throwing up of these secondary products exerts in turn a final influence on the whole, but there is never any doubt as to which is prior.

Because laws, sciences, languages, arts, distribution systems, moralities and all the social relations and status arrangements connected therewith, are as it were the most generalised, the most social, the most recent, and the furthest removed from nature of all economic products, they form the superstructure or most abstract portion of history. They form the theory of human life, the consciousness of society, the visible flower of activity; but they grow from, are nourished by, and are a new aspect of living, breathing, working, active men. If men in the course of their interaction with nature, living practically as men in nature and in society, are faced with an objective fact that contradicts this social theory of life, a tension is generated which will ultimately bring about the appropriate modification of the superstructure. Moreover, because it is a social or shared superstructure, only those facts will bring about its modification which are capable of being made social facts, facts connected with man's relation as associated man to outer reality. We may say if we like that minor transformations of technique ultimately affect the whole superstructure. Or we may say with more detail that when associated men immediately in interaction with nature discover discrepancies between theory and practice, immediate detailed theory is modified accordingly—('technological improvement')—and as the minor discrepancies accumulate, theories more and more general or 'social' in scope are affected, until ultimately the whole superstructure is modified—'ideological development'.

This is the evolutionary theory of society, which holds good for all society that has any consciousness and is at grips with nature; but the two are the same—conscious man is socially productive man. This theory is therefore the basic theory of human society. It is the fundamental law of motion of history, and applies to all men's theories and to all men's activities. Necessarily, because it is a scientific theory, it sees history as still being made now and all men's contemporary theories and activities as part of the science of history. History can only find the theoretical past in the theoretical present and can only develop the theoretical present by being active, and so producing the real future.

In the history of evolution, Marx also discovered revolution. He found, as a well-known objective fact, that instead of the superstructure being always gradually, by small increments, remodelled by men's daily activity, there were periods when the whole superstructure, as if with explosive force, was rapidly shattered and transformed. Laws, sciences, arts, rights, distribution systems—all were involved in one stupendous explosion, lasting for one or two centuries, like the slow motion film of a bursting bomb.

Now this could only mean one thing, that for some reason an insulating gap had opened between the superstructure (theory) and the basis (practice) so that practice could not continually modify theory. As a result the antagonism had grown and the tension had at last become so terrific that the resultant explosion had shattered almost every portion of the old superstructure. An obvious example was the bourgeois revolution which inaugurated the 'modern era'.

But why (Marx asked) should revolutions be? Why should the superstructure show this rigidity, and permit an explosive antagonism to be generated in society?

Marx's answer was one of the most revelatory hypotheses ever framed. *The antagonism is itself only a reflection in the ideological sphere of a fundamental division in production, and this division is expressed, in the sphere of social relations, by antagonistic classes, of which one class is the conscious, contemplative, directing, and therefore ruling class and the other is the unconscious active, directed and ruled class.* Therefore the antagonism between conscious superstructure and active technique is an antagonism which reflects the division of society's economic production. One class directs economic production consciously and by so doing is able to direct the flow of the bulk of society's economic products into its life. The other class is directed and exploited. The directive, conscious class is the class that produces the consciousness of society: *the superstructure is the product of the exploiting class.*

But the exploited class is the class that performs the actual labour; it is the class which is directly at grips with nature; it is the class which handles the productive forces of society. The ruling class only came into being because its members performed a socially useful function, by directing labour they increased the productive efficiency of society as a whole. The first stages of such a class society are therefore an increase in productive forces because of the new class structure. The society flourishes.

But as the society develops the class antagonism develops. There is a growing division between thinking and acting, between the exploiters and exploited. Theory flies apart from practice; the ruling class become less functional, and more parasitic, contemplative and idealistic, and the exploited class more and more become the sole controllers of the productive forces of society at the same time as they become more and more divorced from its products. The productive forces as they develop indicate the increasing technical power of man and his increasing practical experience of reality, but since the productive forces are the domain of the exploited, and the theory or superstructure is the creation of the exploiting class, there is only generated a growing antagonism between theory and practice, evident in an increasing divorce of man's professions from reality, and of the outward forms of society from its true content. There is an increase in exploitation, in the parasitical rôle of the exploiting class, and a growing contradiction between what man could do and what he is actually doing. Man thinks fine things and does hateful ones. He is 'sinful', base, and degenerate, at the very time when his notions are most highfalutin.

This antagonism cannot but continue to develop, for every growth in productive forces exposes the faults of the superstructure and, at the same time, makes the non-productive class cling more closely to it. The superstructure now becomes transformed through the necessities of maintaining the class division which begot it, and it becomes transformed into a class-fortress and base for reaction, counter-revolution and Fascism—thus adding to the bitterness of the struggle. Revolution occurs when the exploited class, operating the productive forces of society, revolts and shatters the whole superstructure that crippled it.

This revolt is not a blind shattering. The exploited class, in control of the productive forces, has by its very development of those forces learned the new technique which negates the superstructure of the exploiting class. Because theory and practice have got into antagonistic hands, each development of productive forces could not transform the superstructure in an evolutionary manner, but these developments accumulated until they attained explosive force. Thus, by the time a revolutionary situation has matured, there is a whole new superstructure latent in the exploited class, arising from all they have learned from the development of productive forces, and this becomes the starting point for the superstructure of the new society, which therefore is one which starts on a higher plane than that of the overthrown society. This is the creative rôle of revolutions. It is shown clearly in the bourgeois revolution, where the exploited class of the towns, the bourgeoisie, because of the development as productive forces of bourgeois private property, overthrew the feudal regime with its superstructure based on status or degree, and established one based on private property.

The proletarian revolution is a consequence of the increasing antagonism between bourgeois superstructure and proletarian labour, and when the crippling by the superstructure of the productive forces—visible in slumps, poverty, war and unemployment—grows unbearable, not only does the proletariat revolt but the very technical developments which increased its productivity—social organisation of production *inside* the unit—also generates the ideology which transforms the capitalist superstructure. The proletarian superstructure is, long before the revolution in Russia, already extant in embryo in the form of Marxism or scientific socialism, and this is in turn the product of the analysis by Marx of capitalist production. In this analysis of the past history of society in contemporary capitalism, he saw the new productive forces made possible by the proletarianisation of labour, and only realisable in communism.

Thus Marx was able to answer the question as to why the superstructure becomes detached from the foundations, and society is rent in twain. It is the result of a class cleavage. He was able to show that these classes themselves only arose as a development of special forms of production—the slave with agricultural production, the bourgeois with feudal production, and the proletarian with capitalist production; and he was able also to show how the transformation of the superstructure, the accompaniment of revolution, was not an arbitrary shattering, but the realisation in new social relations of possibilities already latent in practice.

The same analysis answers our original question, why the bourgeois sciences, for all their achievement, are unable to create a synthetic ideology but by their very development bring about the disintegration of bourgeois culture. Sciences are ultimately in empirical contact with reality; they have a technical, practical basis. This differentiates science from mere theory. This practical basis is the front, as it were, along which science advances, and the new matter it encounters should travel up to the superstructure and modify it. But, as we have seen, the superstructure or 'world-view' of a culture is the creation of a ruling class which becomes increasingly divorced from practice, increasingly self-illusory and non-functional. An antagonism therefore arises between this central ideology and the advancing practical front of science, which results in a crippling and distortion of science in proportion as it becomes generalised, and approaches wide theoretical formulations. As a result science is repelled by the central ideology, and gathers itself round its most practical fronts which thus become closed worlds—detached and isolated sciences. This has as a further result the separation of the world-view from the sciences, with its ensuing collapse and disintegration, and the impoverishment of the now isolated, separate sciences.

Since classes are not arbitrary absolute creations, but come into being as specific developments of economy, they are by no means inevitable. The exploitation relationship is not essential to society, and Marx showed that the proletariat in fact occupied the special historical position of the class destined to end classes, to bring about its own extinction as a class.

Since the bourgeoisie, once expropriated, has no social status, it must cease to exist, and then the coercive content of the State superstructure vanishes. Only one class is left—that is to say, there are no classes—and this class both owns and operates the productive forces of society. There is no longer a fundamental cleavage between theory and practice, which now can affect each other directly and rapidly, and each innovation in practice can at once affect the superstructure.

Such a conception of history not only exposed the fundamental law of motion of social men, but it also reinstated history as a science like other sciences, that is, one in which practice is the ally of theory and *vice-versa*. No more than it is possible to separate the science of chemistry from laboratory experiments, or that of cosmogony from physical experiments, is it possible to separate history, which is the apex of the sciences, from social activity. History then becomes, not merely a study of inscriptions and records and witnesses, but the means of answering questions which were in olden days phrased in such symbolic forms as: 'What is my duty to my neighbour?' 'What is man's destiny?' 'Why is Truth independent of me?' 'What is the worth of Beauty?' 'What must I do to be saved?' 'Is Evil real?' History becomes, just because it is the study of the past in the present, the guide to the future. Since future history is made only by the present actions of men, as they realise themselves, such a history must necessarily be a guide to action now. And each such action, by establishing or modifying or enriching the content of the science of history, also increases its penetrative power in analyses of the past, and enables it with increasing success to separate the past from that present in which the past is implicit.

Thus Marx and Engels not only explained the movement of history, they also made history real and scientific by making it a guide to man's action in relation to society now. Because we, in a bourgeois world, live in a time when the superstructure of the bourgeois class cripples the productive powers of organised labour, historical materialism is a guide to our action in changing this superstructure and participating in the proletarian revolution. Of course it is just this in Marxism that scandalises the bourgeoisie—it is an historical *science*, and is therefore warm and breathing. Historical materialism is not a mere dead congelation of knowledge of the past, as if the past were something separate from the present and outside it, or as if the social activities of all men who went before us were altogether external to us, instead of being forces in a movement of which we are the momentary apex and culmination. It is the past active in the present and aiding man actively to produce the future.

IV

CONSCIOUSNESS

A Study in Bourgeois Psychology

1

IT is characteristic of bourgeois psychology that it is confused and inconclusive in its treatment of what would seem, to many people, the most important subject of psychological study, consciousness. Bourgeois psychology has a choice between six doctrines about consciousness, and it will throw light on the difficulties with which that psychology is faced if we detail them:—

(*a*) Consciousness contains the sole data of psychology (philosophical and faculty psychologies).

(*b*) Consciousness is an epiphenomenon accompanying neurological activity (neurological psychology and psychophysiology).

(*c*) Consciousness plays no causal part in behaviour, which can be completely described and determined without its use. Since behaviour is the only thing that can be observed in others, the existence of consciousness should on principles of epistemology be denied (behaviourism).

(*d*) The psyche consists of the products of one or a number of transformed instincts; some of these products are conscious, others are unconscious (Freudism and its derivatives; and 'hormic' psychology).

(*e*) Consciousness consists of the shuffling of forms of thought according to dynamical laws (association psychology and gestalt psychology).

(*f*) In so far as any or all of the above theories produce empirically-proven results, they are right (eclectic or academic psychology).

It sounds a hopeless muddle, and in fact it is a muddle without hope as long as psychologists move within the circle of bourgeois philosophy. Yet would anyone familiar with contemporary psychology accuse me of overstating the case? It is in fact usual to provide many more classifications: for example a gestalt psychologist would insist on being separated from the old-fashioned associationist and the Freudian from the adherent of McDougall, and the follower of Jung or Adler from both.

It is obvious that all these schools cannot be right. For example (*a*) and (*c*) also (*d*) and (*e*) are exclusive opposites. It is as near certain as anything can be that none of them is right. There is no more depressing spectacle in bourgeois culture to-day than this of a science so important and vital to human knowledge as psychology unable to secure agreement about the most elementary feature of its domain. But may not this be a necessary feature of psychology itself which perhaps, as some scientists have suggested, can never be a science; and is not this more likely than that the failure of its psychology should be a necessary characteristic of bourgeois culture?

The answer is, that not only is the anarchy of psychology a necessary feature of bourgeois culture, but that the very attitude of mind which supposes that psychology can never be a science, is itself an outcome of the same fundamental position. Bourgeois psychology grew out of biology through the influence of physiology on philosophy; but equally bourgeois physics affects it, for it determines on the one hand bourgeois philosophy and on the other hand bourgeois biology. Medicine, too, throws its contribution into psychology through physiology and it is chiefly philosophical medicine, medicine formulated in terms of the current bourgeois philosophy.

Does this sound an inextricable tangle, accounting for the confusion of psychology, the latest of the empirically developed sciences? It does so only because the bourgeois sciences, as an outcome of the bourgeois position, cannot be conceived except as either confusing or dominating each other. Either the fundamental categories of 'the sciences' are held to be exclusive, and nothing can result from their combination except a mish-mash *or*, alternatively, one science excludes and suppresses the categories of the others, as in behaviourism, the categories of bourgeois biology are allowed to suppress those proper to psychology, and in mechanical materialism the categories of bourgeois physics are allowed to usurp those of all other spheres of science. *Either* the spheres of the positive sciences are distinct, *or* they are the same, that is the dilemma which bourgeois science has posed for itself, and it can never imagine that they are different and yet mutually determinative.

The bourgeois, by his fundamental position, is free 'in himself'. He is free not because he is conscious of his causality, but because he is ignorant of the social causes that determine his being. He pictures himself therefore as standing in a dominating relation to his environment, just as in society he seems by his dominating relation to capital and his ownership of social labour power, to be determining society and not determined by it.

He is in fact deluded, for his ownership of capital does not enable him consciously to determine society even though his actions determine its fate. The sum of bourgeois wills produces history, but it is not the history any one bourgeois willed. His efforts for one thing produce another thing—his attempts at profit produce loss, at plenty poverty, at peace war. As his culture collapses all his efforts to shore it up hasten that collapse. He finds himself unfree after all, although he is 'in control' of social forces.

Why then was he unfree? Where did he err? He erred because he did not see that his dominating relation to society was a determining relation, which determined him as much as he determined it. He was unconscious of this, and therefore unable to achieve freedom. His conception of freedom really arose as a special case of a group of illusions about domination which has been associated with all forms of society based on dominating classes. This group of illusions has for a common factor the belief that domination secures self-determination. But it follows from the material unity of the Universe that this is untrue. All the phenomena that constitute the universe are mutually determined. If any group were completely self-determined it would constitute a closed world, and would not exist. All relations are determining. The earth appears to primitive man to dominate the cosmos—sun and stars appear to rotate round it. This is a pleasant illusion, but it does not make us astronomers, much less does it make us people round whom the cosmos revolves. As soon as we realise there is a determining relation, and become conscious of its nature and how it grips us, we are that much freer of cosmic phenomena, and can predict eclipses, construct sidereal time, navigate, and govern our actions according to the necessity of the Universe.

All previous cultures that were ideologically conscious at all have been based on a ruling class which consciously dominated and directed the utilisation of productive forces. As a result all such cultures were subject to an illusion distorting their ideologies. Slave-owning culture conceived freedom to consist in this, in the domination of the will of one man over the will of another, the other passively obeying this one's will. This gives rise to the *teleological* explanation of the Universe, which reaches its subtlest form in Plato's or Aristotle's philosophies, in which all phenomena are determined by Ideas or Forms. These correspond to the plans formed in the mind of the slave-owner which his slave passively fulfils. This explanation applies equally to social and non-social phenomena, and therefore is consistent. The domination inherent in the slave-owning system is not repressed, as with the bourgeois, but is conscious, and the illusion consists, not in supposing that no domination exists, but that society is in fact really determined solely by the will of the master, and does not in turn determine his will. This will, which therefore appears as the first cause in society just because it is conscious, also appears the first cause in the Universe, as the Law of the Universe, as the doctrine of Ends, Final Causes, Perfect Ideas (willed by one or more supreme causes or Divine Masters) whose plans the Universe fulfils and thus develops.

Society is not in fact determined by the will of a slave-owning master, but by the productive forces at the service of such an economy. The master's will is itself determined by the society in which he finds himself and, just because he is unconscious of these causes, the slave owner is unfree. His world of ends is inadequate, not only as a basis for sociology, but also for physics, biology and psychology. It cannot exhibit true causal relations: only demons disguised as final causes. The slave-owning world, incapable of being deeply scientific or analytical, inevitably marches on to the Empire, whose fiction it is that the whole Empire's activity is controlled by the will of one master, the Emperor. And this Empire as inevitably marches on to ruin, for the productive forces are not controlled by the will of the Emperor but instead, crippled by slave-owning productive relations, the Imperial economy decays for all his efforts, and it is a world whose income has steadily diminished, whose soil is impoverished and whose people is demoralised, that crumbles at any push from the barbarians so easily repelled at the height of the Empire's power.

No less than the slave-owning, the feudal civilisation is in the grip of the illusion of dominion. The dominion is still conscious, as it is in slave-owning civilisation, and therefore necessarily gives rise to a physics and to a world-view in which all causes are final causes—conscious purposes in the mind of a dominating master. In this respect it simply takes over Aristotelianism, the most consistent expression of slave-owning philosophy. But now this domination is regarded as necessarily exercised according to a hierarchy of privilege; the day of unrestricted property in slaves is over. The dominating relation is exercised 'according to law', and this law itself is only the reflection of the Roman technical apparatus of learning, social organisation, and administrative skill taken over with the Church from the Empire by the barbarian overlords. This technical apparatus becomes symbolised as Christendom, as the monopoly of the Church, as benefit of clergy, as an instrument which must be used to sanction all acts of domination. from kingship to knighthood. Aristotelianism must therefore be modified: and while final causes are still the explanatory mechanism these final causes are, in Scholasticism and Thomism, causes which are established by a law of God, which can only work themselves out according to a fiat given forth at the Creation. The world works according to God-sanctioned laws which have a purpose, and have had a purpose from the beginning of time. These laws are not self-driving, but require the continual impetus of deity. They can therefore be suspended at any time by the Divine Will, but such miracles are rare.

Science therefore in feudal civilisation is still in embryo but it is yet a stage nearer birth than in slave-owning society.

A dominion which, in addition to the free will of the master, requires also the sanction of the impersonal law, is already well on the way to be determined, even if it is determined from above by another dominating will—God's. A world ruled by law is well on the way to being a world ruled by causality.

In a sense this is an accident. Feudal law is only the Imperial law of slave-owning society preserved through the survival of Roman economy in the monastery-farm, example to the barbarian of agricultural efficiency and therefore the ancestor of the manor. But the fact of this survival changes it. In Roman society, law's sanction is simply this, that it expresses the will of the Divine Emperor, who owns his people like a slave-owner. To medieval society, to the barbarian invader, law comes as something outside the will of the ruler, as an impersonal and pre-existing body of law, as Christendom, with which he must comply if the social production from which he draws tribute is to be carried on, for that production functions according to these laws, and otherwise collapses in anarchy. The law therefore appears, not as a fiat of any serf-owner's will but as something determining in some measure the range of will of both serf and serf owner, a something existent from the beginning of time. Hence feudal society provides the necessary transition to the bourgeois position.

This transition is achieved within the limits of its own illusion by bourgeois culture. The scholastic world laws are stripped of their final causes and become self-driving, while the question of the reason for and time of their issue by the Creator is postponed or treated as outside the province of science. Science is thus conceived for the first time as the field of laws which connect phenomena in a mutually determining way, and are sufficiently explained by exhibiting the structure of that determinism. These laws do not require as their sanction a final cause nor a clearly expressed divine *place in the cosmos* and do not therefore explain nature as the vehicle of conscious wills exercising dominion.

This ought to be the death of animism. Animism is nothing but the attribution to nature, as the sufficient cause of all phenomena, of human wills, due to the primitive's illusion that the will is a freely determining cause in itself, and not in the act of willing itself determined. In primitive communism, where there is no domination or division of labour, such wills seem present in every individual freely determining his behaviour as a cause, and therefore by analogy they are held to play the same part in the beneficent or maleficent activities of trees, stones, and stars, which obey their own wills without overlords. But the slave-owner is well aware that though the slave may will as he please, the slave's will is not the cause of the slave's activities, which are caused by his master's will. He therefore subtilises animism to this extent, that trees and stones have not wills of their own, but are passive subjects to a god's will:

> From haunted spring, and dale
> Edg'd with poplar pale,
> The parting Genius is with sighing sent,
> With flowre-inwov'n tresses torn
> The Nimphs in twilight shade of tangled thickets
> mourn.

So early Greek animism, with the development of its economy, gives place to the teleology of Aristotle.

The slave-owner is at times visited with a nightmare. He finds that his free will, in spite of its freedom, is thwarted, not by a superior will but by things-in-themselves—by inferior wills, accidents, mistakes, and his own ignorance. Yet he is still unable to conceive his will except as being thwarted like that of his slave's by another will, and since he the master is so thwarted, might not even the world's master and his—God Himself—be thwarted in his volition by some grand over-riding will, by Will-in-Itself? This is the slave-owning conception of Moira, or Fate, a comparatively late development reaching its noblest expression in Greek tragedy. This Fate, in spite of its closeness to bourgeois determinism, betrays its slave-owning parentage by the fact that it is always visualised as a consciously foreseeing Will, and always as thwarting, not determining human wills *as well as* events, but *interfering* with human wills *by means of* events.

Animism, slave-owning teleology and Fate, feudal teleology and Law, these then are the steps by which society in its development explains the world. It was the rôle of the bourgeois to carry a step forward, not only society's productive development but also and necessarily also its explanation of the Universe.

* * * * *

The bourgeois first finds himself as one of a class whose development is restricted by feudal privilege and the reign of law imposed by Christendom. He therefore revolts against it and, in the circumstances in which he finds himself, he necessarily formulates his case as follows:—

(i) The dominating relations of one man over another are evil, and must be eliminated, for they hold up productive forces (that is, the productive forces of my class).

(ii) Law is not something immutable existing from the beginning of time and imposed on men from without. Any such imposed law is wrong. A man's law is in himself. What seems to him in the given circumstances best or proper to do, is right, and there should be no other law.

This means that the bourgeois turns Catholic dogma into personal Protestantism, and that all feudal laws, monopolies, or privileges which restrict his doing what seems best to himself, are abolished in the course of his revolution. Those restrictive laws are, however, all laws interfering with his right to acquire, alienate and own capital. He does not however regard this right as a 'law', but as something given in the nature of things, and in his own nature.

The bourgeois thus emerges to consciousness as a man whose views of the world are determined by social causes, just like the slave-owner or lord. Freedom consists in this, in each man's doing what seems best to himself, consulting, not some good laid down by law like the service to his overlord by which the feudal landowner held his land, but his own good. Out of this apparent confusion of personal competition will emerge (according to the bourgeois) a world-order that is the best possible, because it is the product of freedom. To this illusion the bourgeois is completely committed by his revolutionary programme.

But as I explained elsewhere, * this society, in spite of its apparent individual freedom, is still based on a dominating relation. The bourgeois as the source of uncontrolled free activity in society, must necessarily be uncontrolled in his ownership of social capital. This apparently innocent dominating relation to a thing also involves, after all, dominion over men, just as in previous societies, but unlike the ruling class in previous societies the bourgeois cannot consciously assert dominion over other wills as a law of society; on the contrary he is committed to repress the knowledge or deny the existence of such a law. Moreover the very dominion thus exercised imposes a conflict in society between the haves and have-nots, which would become overt and suicidal to society if it were not forcibly repressed and kept harmless, not once and for all, but as

* *V.* 'Pacifism and Violence' in *Studies in a Dying Culture.*

long as the antagonising domination exists, which is as long as culture remains bourgeois.

Thus after a bourgeois revolution, the resultant strife is suppressed by a 'strong man' who forcibly imposes a coercive law on haves and have-nots alike, making possible unrestricted capitalism. In English history this strong man is, after the bourgeois Reformation, the Tudor monarch, and, after the Revolution, Cromwell. In France he is Napoleon. But this 'strong man', though necessary, is by bourgeois standards himself an anomaly, and as soon as he has called into being laws protecting bourgeois rights, he is eliminated in favour of a rubber stamp monarch (the Glorious Revolution of England) or a President (France) and the bourgeois task then becomes simply the preservation of this body of law in its main principles (the constitution, democracy, etc.) with the incorporation of such minor amendments as social development renders necessary (legislation). These laws are now hypostatised as the essence of liberty and justice (freedom and parliamentary democracy).

How is this change reflected in the world of science, with which we are concerned? The world of science follows the same course. The first attempt at a bourgeois world-view as homogeneous as that of Aristotle or Thomas Aquinas necessarily fails from the outset by reason of this split in the bourgeois position. Either classicism or feudalism can achieve a homogeneous world-view in a far more consistent anticipation of Schopenhauer's philosophy: the 'World as Will and Idea' (or rather, as Will and *Aim*). And, unlike Schopenhauer's, such a world-view expresses in a refined form the viewpoint of all thinking men in that culture. This the bourgeois never achieves.

He is divided between two contradictory points of view. In himself he is exempt from determinism, not because of the dominating relation of his class to society (as with classical society) but through the absence of any conscious relation to other men at all. Other men neither dominate him nor are dominated by him (he thinks), and the ideal society, to which all bourgeois strive, is one in which each unit is insulated, and the world of society and of values drives on in the best possible way as the result of the independent, self-motivated action of every free bourgeois.

At the same time he stands, as owner and master of social capital, in a dominating relation to 'Nature', his environment. Social capital is the crystallisation of men's attempts to control nature through their empirical knowledge of its causality. He is in charge of this manipulation of nature, but this is not a relation of will like that of classical society, for the bourgeois by his position is committed to the belief that a dominating relation to a thing (private property) is not a dominating relation at all. It is therefore a relation in which will does not enter in the sense that to will a thing is to have the slave do it if it is do-able, and if not—well, slaves are not perfect and it is not for the master to do the slave's business for him. It is a new kind of relation in which the bourgeois as it were 'administers' a thing, so as to draw out from its intrinsic qualities the maximum benefit to society, which, in bourgeois language, appears translated as 'the maximum profit to himself'. Of course he is not really administering property, he is exploiting labour power.

Unlike the classic or feudal position, such a position is from the outset self-contradictory, and will never be able to generate a consistent world-view; dualism is implicit in it. For from the bourgeois point of view, in the world of society freedom seems to inhere in the individual will unconscious of any causality or outer necessity; but in the world of nature, freedom seems to inhere in the drawing-out by the will of the necessary qualities in Nature and, therefore, in consciousness of the necessity of Nature. The first view is completely fallacious; but the second is nearer reality than a teleological explanation, and therefore bourgeois culture is culture which gives birth for the first time to a science of the environment of nature, a thing almost unknown to previous cultures. Nonetheless, the fundamental fallacy of this position means that increasing success in the second, or scientific, world view will add to the inconsistency and anarchy of the first; and ultimately the second world view will itself become affected, for both are only abstractions from the one reality.

* * * * *

We have in other essays explored different aspects of the disintegration of bourgeois science; here we merely concentrate on the duel between physics and psychology. The bourgeois looked round on his social world and unconsciously projected it into the world of physics, into his environment. He therefore discovered new truths about his environment, for the world of society is a part of reality. But, coming back to society, he could not, because the projection was unconscious, see society as determined in the way the world of physics was determined, for to do so would be to make social necessity conscious. He stood in his own light. As a bourgeois he had been unconscious of any necessity determining his action, for the bourgeois law for social action is 'Do as you will'. It forgets to state whether (*a*) you *can* do as you will; (*b*) you can *will* what you will.

Hence the world of physics, in which the 'wills' of the particles are determined at first by God but later by the relations of the particles themselves, would have been the basis of an accurate view of bourgeois society, but the bourgeois was unable to achieve it. He kept on getting near it, but always this fundamental conviction that his will and desires were the source of social motion prevented it. If on the one hand he saw society as a network of determining relations and, on the other hand, his own mind as determined by this, he would have seen that not only did society produce from its interaction 'laws of supply and demand', but that his conceptions of justice and right were also determined by society. But this last step he could never make, for to him his own self was the source of the free energy which, interacting with bourgeois society, gave rise to economic law.

This failure meant that he conceived his desires and notions of justice, morality and so forth, as not in any way determined, but as primary and therefore eternal. Necessarily, the type of society of which these were the outcome was the eternal type of society—any deviation was either discredited or was an accident.

This results in three different worlds which are of major importance in understanding the distortion of bourgeois thought.

(i) *The world of physics.* This world, modelled on bourgeois society unconsciously grasped in experience by the bourgeois, is a world of particles trading freely with each other and giving rise to laws of supply and demand which dictate the behaviour of the world as a whole. Because nature is not a dominated slave, but an administered thing, it is non-living and non-mental: a-teleological therefore and stripped of all quality.

It is a closed world, which does not interact with the bourgeois, who surveys it to learn its laws and use it like a machine—hence it is in absolute space and time, independent of the observing mind. In order that it should not be in determining relation with mind, it is by definition bare of all qualities found in mind (the so-called sensory or secondary qualities). But these ultimately are found to include *all* material qualities. Consequently the bourgeois closed world of physics, by definition restricted to matter, which matter is defined as 'non-mind', becomes barer and barer of real qualities until 'nothing' is left. But something must be left—there are the concepts that describe the 'structure' of this nothing. Thus mechanical materialism by its very premises is pushed on to become its apparent opposite, mentalism, which it reaches with Mach, Eddington, Jeans, and their followers.

The closed world of matter, restricted to non-mental qualities, is bound to collapse. 'Pure' physics is bound to reveal itself as an illusion. This it does by flying into two contradictory halves. On the one hand absolute space and time, independent of the observer, is saved by fusing them (space-time) and using the elaborate apparatus of the tensor to eliminate the determining effect of the observer and close the world by making it 'invariant for all transformations'. On the other hand this is flatly contradicted by quantum mechanics, which is composed partly of matrices of *observations alone*, partly of waves in absolute time-space which *are not however waves of matter* but waves indicating the *probability* of matter being present. In both cases matter is supposed to lurk behind the numbers as an unknowable Ding-an-sich.

(ii) *The closed world of sociology.* Here, once again, the bourgeois surveys a world from outside, and since his mind is not determined by it, though he lives in it, the social concepts in his mind are eternal (the laws of appetite, supply and demand, justice, free trade, etc.). These concepts therefore function in the world of sociology as laws regulating the free clash of individuals, and not as products of certain stages of that clash. Consequently, as in the famous mercantile examples, if two men meet on a desert island, their transactions strangely enough always and inevitably produce bourgeois economics, and this is taken as a proof of the validity of the bourgeois concepts. It follows from this that although the bourgeois can give a fairly accurate picture of contemporary sociology, it is a static picture, and neglects the vital laws of motion. Pigou can seriously devote a book to 'The Economics of a Stationary State'. Hence—not only is all bourgeois economics false as a science, and therefore as a guide to prediction and action, but it cannot give a deterministic and causal picture of the development of society in all its varieties of culture. Thus the closed world of bourgeois sociology is far less accurate than the closed world of physics. Both are absolute, but whereas in the history of man the environment does not to any degree alter, society itself alters rapidly, and thus bourgeois culture precludes itself from writing a scientific history of any feature of its culture from economics to religion. Yet change manifestly occurs and therefore some force must be invoked from an outside world to produce these changes. On the one hand ludicrously simple causes from spheres anterior to the sociological will be brought in as sufficiently explanatory —climatic changes, racial differences, differential birthrate dietetic deficiencies (Marett), or, on the other hand, causes from spheres posterior to the sociological will be used in explaining the change—great Ideas, the invention of steam, the concept of liberty (H. A. Fisher), a cycle of flourishing and decay (Spengler). Both forms of explanation are equally unscientific but are preferred by the bourgeois to admitting that he is unconsciously determined by social relations, and that the 'fundamental' categories he has carefully established for sociology, are simply the product of his own particular phase of social relations.

(iii) *The closed world of psychology.* It was inevitable that the bourgeois should excel himself when he came to establish the categories of his own mind. The closed world of psychology is as it were the antithesis of the closed world of physics. Now if we abstract from mind all 'material' qualities we travel the reverse road to bourgeois physics and we end up with something that contains no qualities at all. That is to say, consciousness is 'nothing'. But mind exists and the brain exists, therefore mind is simply physical matter in its sensory aspects, *the behaviour of the body.* Thus whilst in physics the bourgeois recipe for matter, 'not-mind,' was producing a matter so stripped of all material qualities as to evaporate into mind (cp. Eddington, Jeans and Russell); in psychology the bourgeois recipe for mind, 'not-matter,' was producing a mind so stripped of all mental qualities that it solidified into matter, and became behaviourism. These two doctrines, so apparently opposed, produce each other, and follow from the one bourgeois position.

Before this, however, the bourgeois standpoint had succeeded in generating all the other distortions of psychology we have listed at the beginning of this essay. The simplest bourgeois position is that, since mind is not determined and is therefore free, the laws of the mind can only be studied in its products. But to consciousness, mind's products are all conscious products. Only the world of consciousness exists for psychology and, by this definition, psychology is the study not merely of non-material but of 'non-unconscious' qualities of the mind.

The first attempts at this form of bourgeois psychology are systematic. They are merely the classification of conscious phenomena (Faculty psychology). Since the psychological field is undetermined there is no reason why faculties should not be anything, and as a result they are merely subsumed according to the prejudices of the moment and the structure of language at the time.

But it is impossible by reason of the very nature of knowledge that any field can be depicted as indetermined within itself, for every positive statement must necessarily express some kind of determinism. The most the bourgeois position claims is that mental phenomena are, in their own sphere, self-determined. The next step from faculty psychology is therefore the study of the self-determination of psychological products. The bourgeois, freely wandering about the world he dominates, acquires images of it or ideas, and these interact and live their lives, and combine and move by virtue of causal laws, parallel to but different from those that rule the world of particles in the closed world of physics. This closed world of Ideas, foreshadowed in Locke, reaches its final development in the associationists, with whom everything is explained by the 'association of ideas'. It still represents an important influence in all modern psychologies, for it appears to solve the problem of the closed worlds by creating two parallel worlds, quite in the manner of Descartes.

But unfortunately biology, itself a closed world, here erupts to shatter this dream of the parallel worlds, one of physics in which particles move according to physical laws, and the other of conscious ideas in which images of the real world move according to mental 'laws'. Biology, in human physiology, discovers a connecting link breaking into both worlds. On the one hand the body is composed of particles subject to physical laws, on the other hand, as aphasia and cerebral injuries show, disturbance of particles of the body leads to a disturbance of 'ideas'. The two absolute worlds must be joined.

This is the function of neurology. To neurology, however delicately its practisers may veil their position, the nerves (and particularly the cerebral neurones) are subject to electrical disturbances or waves of potential variation as the result of stimuli, and these waves are accompanied by ideas, just as the passage of an electric current across two poles in the atmosphere is accompanied by a spark. Great success is achieved by neurology in its correlation of conscious with physiological phenomena.

In this way mind is forced into the closed world of physics. The particles still move about in absolute time and space (for few, if any, neurologists have advanced to Einstein's absolute time-space) but now their movements are accompanied by a kind of iridescence or glow, which is mind.

The closed world of physics is a world dominated by the bourgeois, viewing it from outside and therefore able to foresee, by a Divine Calculation, the whole course of future movements of particles. This is bourgeois *pre*determinism, in which the whole future ean be imagined as consciously known in its necessary future evolution, like the movements of a machine, just as in slave-owning fatalism the whole future can be imagined as consciously planned. In the former case the necessity arises from the causality of things; in the latter from the will of the planner; but in both cases the predestination consists in the conscious pre-knowledge of events.

But if consciousness itself is—as it evidently is—a late development of the Universe, such a conception falls to the ground. And if mind is also part of the network of determinism, each act of knowing involved in consciousness plays a determining as well as a determined rôle, and the mere fact of being all-knowing like Laplace's divine calculator, would involve a new determining force not allowed for in the original act of knowledge.

To the bourgeois the world of physics has its lines laid down irrespective of mind; it exists *absolutely*. When facts force him to include mind in this already complete, self-driving world, it is therefore simply dragged round with the machinery. Mind becomes pointless and redundant. What the bourgeois thought was the 'ennoblement' of mind—its separation as a distinct thing from gross matter—is in fact its degradation, for now it becomes involved in the mindless causality of bourgeois physics, a causality abstracted of mental qualities, though consciously envisaged as a whole by impersonal Mind. Consciousness is to this abstract Mind an irrelevant phenomenon arising from the predetermined clash of particles.

Nothing could in fact be more repugnant to the bourgeois than this logical outcome of his contradictory position. Therefore bourgeois causality, or predeterminism (the only form of determinism he understands), is the bourgeois nightmare, and it induces him to lead an attack in full force on determinism or causality in physics (Jeans, Eddington, Weyl, Born, *et al*). It leads him at last to picture, by whatever immoral stratagem, the movements of the particles as indetermined; and the particles themselves as unknowable. This he supposes, at last secures his menaced free-will. But in fact free-will does not lie along this road at all.

* * * * *

Thus the neurological approach is the most fruitful to-day in scientific results, yet it is also the most destructive to bourgeois psychology and bourgeois self-esteem. Mind is a material quality, and therefore all mental phenomena are necessarily phenomena displayed by material neurones. But by 'matter' the neurologist does not understand real sensuous matter, for he is a bourgeois physicist, and moreover in most cases a Newtonian bourgeois physicist. He only understands matter as it appears in the bourgeois closed world of physics, stripped of mental qualities, a completely self-determined world excluding mind as expressing a determining relation. Therefore neurological data, growing in certainty and precision, seem more and more to dissolve psychology into something non-mental and predetermined, until we are ready to believe consciousness is an unimportant illusion. This is necessarily so, for a method of approach that sees colour, for example, as an hallucination, the *real* thing being a wave length, must even more see consciousness as an illusion, the real thing being a moving wave of potential. Thus bourgeois consciousness, in all seriousness (with maudlin regret even) denies its own existence, or, alternatively, if this 'daring' view seems dangerous, as easily and from the same fundamental position, denies the existence of anything else *but* consciousness.

Neurology, like early faculty and associationist psychologies, at first sees the problem in its simplest terms—consciousness or mind on the one hand, and on the other hand the physico-physiological world or matter. The categories of both are regarded as eternal.

Nonetheless, various considerations operate to make this simple dualism more complex. In the field of faculty or associationist psychology there is the problem of memory. Ideas vanish and then return (recollection) and return perhaps changed. But they must have been somewhere meanwhile. Where were they stowed? The answer is 'In the Unconscious'. Needless to say, this is at present no answer. To answer the question 'Where are Ideas when they are not-conscious?' with 'In the not-consciousness' is childish. However, if new laws of the process governing not-consciousness are learned, the answer is the starting point of research, and in modern psychology the Unconscious does therefore mean something.

Neurology is not perplexed by the problem in this form. Ideas, being a chance glow, can come or go, no explanation is needed. The problem here arises in a somewhat different form.

(*a*) The cortex and (*b*) the thalamus, the cerebellum, and the spinal cord represent phylogenetically different stages of the growth of the nervous system, and seem to correspond to different kinds of nervous behaviour—(*a*) voluntary behaviour, or willed response, corresponding to a previously conscious idea; (*b*) reflex behaviour, or innate, automatic, unchanging response to stimuli. These two forms of behaviour are not separate, but all behaviour combines differing proportions of each, and the unit of behaviour seems rather the conditioned reflex, in which an innate pattern has been modified by experience. Voluntary behaviour, in which an 'idea' is at work, is in its purest form still like a conditioned reflex, since pre-existing muscular reflexes must be used in behaviour of any kind, and the 'idea' itself is a product of experience.

Thus neurology becomes the study of the integration or mutual interaction of the phylogenetically different systems of neurones, and of the modification of innate responses by experience. The 'problem' of consciousness is solved by supposing that consciousness is associated with cortical innervations. for man is highly conscious and the cortex is phylogenetically the most recent development of the nervous system. The whole problem is in fact visualised as that of the human machine, quite in the manner of Frederick's physician. The stimuli excite nervous activity, behaviour results, and at the end of the behaviour the machine is in a new position of equilibrium. This is an improvement on the closed world of physics in that it is more sensuous and therefore more material. Behaviour, attention, perception and appetite cannot be written in terms of Principles of Least Action or Lagrange's equations. But man is still subject to predeterminism; he is still merely a part of the closed world of physics surveyed from without. However much neurologists may dislike to admit it, the philosophy of neurology is mechanical materialism even where (as for example with MacCurdy), an amateurish attempt is made to escape into a Platonic doctrine of Ideas controlling formless matter ('Patterns').

* * * * *

Meanwhile gestalt psychology has been making an attempt to reconcile the associationist position with the development, since Mill's time, of neurology. The gestaltists are not, however, neurologists, they do not regard mind as the iridescence accompanying the movement of particles. Since mechanical materialism is not their method of approach the gestalt psychologists are forced into the only other bourgeois alternative—idealism. Gestalt psychology is Platonic idealism.

Needless to say it is not just Platonic idealism, but bourgeois Platonic idealism a.tered by all that has been learned since, and moreover applied, not to a world view but to a very limited field, chiefly so far that of perception. It starts out with an apparently materialistic programme—all mental phenomena to be explained on a purely physico-chemical basis. Now we are familiar with such programmes. Physics had one—'all matter non-mental'—whose logical outcome, to the surprise of no one but the bourgeois, is that all matter proves to be—equations. In the same way, since physics and chemistry result in bourgeois science from similar retrictive programmes, a physico-chemical explanation of mental data must necessarily be dangerous. It turns out to be purely Hegelian. Gestalt psychology is objective Idealism of a kind. The psychological phenomena dealt with are the result of the activation of forms or configurations (gestalten) which are pictured as fields patterned three or even four-dimensionally by variations in potential. Stimuli serve both for the activation and modification of these potential-patterns. But a form or pattern is a *concept.* Is not a concept a late product of consciousness and if so, how can we explain mental phenomena as the result of the activation of more recent products of itself? We must therefore assume the existence of these concepts, or forms, *objectively*. Now this is Platonism if carried out half-heartedly, or Hegelianism, if carried out thoroughly. It is characteristic of the anarchy of bourgeois science that every scientist, in his little province, feels himself at liberty to use for that field only categories which, if applied to the world at large, would seem to him false. The gestalt psychologist is not really a Hegelian. To bourgeois science the closed worlds of modern culture do not seem even a necessary evil; they seem to him part of the method of science, and he feels himself a scientific benefactor in building yet another of them on a small scale.

* * * * *

Meanwhile, apart from neurology and gestalt psychology, another psychology has been growing which, while least scientific in its theory, has the largest empirical content. It is perhaps the most thoroughly bourgeois in spirit and is therefore the most powerful in its influence on contemporary thought. This is the varied field of instinct psychology, of which two schools may be taken as representative: Freud's psycho-analysis and McDougall's 'hormic' psychology. There are about half a dozen others, of which Jung's, Adler's, McCurdy's and Burrow's are the most important.

Both see life as the theatre of an indwelling force or conation (McDougall) or instinct (Freud) which is the free source of life's actions on the static environment. A sharp line is thus drawn between life and not-life, between agent and patient, in which life is always insurgent, creative and changeful, and dead matter always resigned, moulded and eternal.

The drama of the instincts then becomes a kind of

bourgeois novel, in which the heroes are the instincts; and their experiences, mutual struggles and transformations generate not only all psychical but also all cultural phenomena.

Such a view is a fairly accurate description of life as it sees itself in bourgeois consciousness. It is a biological psychology, and therefore makes the same mistake as physical psychology (neurology) and mental psychology (associationism). It dichotomises life and the environment, and defines the environment as all that which possesses no living qualities. The environment is stripped of all qualities common to dead matter and life, and therefore becomes something invariant, ghostly, and unimportant. Everything emerges from within life.

This is the closed world of biology. All change, development, and quality is cooped up within it. Outside is only the Sahara of bourgeois phsyics, quantitative, changeless, bare. All freedom, all self-determination and all motive force therefore comes within the world of life. Change is not a quality of matter but of life. It becomes a special case in the Universe, and therefore inexplicable. The biological dichotomy necessarily leads us, if we expand it, to an uncaused first cause, a Life-Force or vital spirit, which by its ingression in matter makes matter change and develop and therefore living, for change is regarded as a characteristic peculiar to life. Of course instinct psychology does not advance to such a world-view, or press its assumptions to their logical conclusion. It simply takes as a proven thing the closed world of bourgeois biology, and from it extracts the essence of living action, the instincts, which then become the postulates of psychology.

What in fact are these instincts? They are innate patterns of behaviour automatically elicited by stimuli. They are therefore inevitable recurrences amid the sea of change, like the seasons. They are determined in fact (predetermined) by past events. The absoluteness at once reveals them as quantitative abstractions, like energy or space in physics.

But this is not how the bourgeois sees them. He necessarily regards all behaviour that bursts 'spontaneously' forth from the individual ignorant of its causality, as above all free. Therefore the instincts are conceived as freely striving for unconscious goals, and psychology becomes the adventures of the free instincts in their struggles against the restraints of the *environment* (in Freud, of *society*) which impede and cripple their freedom. Out of this struggle cognitive and emotional consciousness is born.

Now the only objection to this bourgeois psychology is that it inverts the picture. The instincts are not free springs of connation towards a goal. They are, so far as they can be abstractly separated, unconscious necessities, as Kant realised. They are unfree. But in their realisation as behaviour, when these innate things-in-themselves become things-for-themselves and interact with their environment (which also changes, and is not the dead world of physics) they also change. Above all, they are changed in human culture. As a result of this change, these necessities become conscious, become emotion and thought; they exist for themselves and are altered thereby. The change *is* the emotion or thought, and now they are no longer the instincts, for they are conscious and consciousness is not an ethereal but a material determining relationship. The necessity that is conscious is not the necessity that is unconscious. The conscious goal is different from the blind 'instinctive' goal. It is freer.

But how can bourgeois instinct psychology grasp this? The magnificent story of human culture becomes in its view simply the tragedy of the crippling of the free instincts by the social restraints they have freely created. The creation of these social restraints is arbitrary, non-causal and pointless, so that history remains thoroughly bourgeois and indetermined; and each psycho-analyst can give a different explanation of any sociological phenomenon. Experience, art and science are in this psychology the fetters of the instinctive energy; all experiences are the scars of the wounds to this freedom (inhibition and repression). Moreover the unconscious plays a strange role. Since experience is in this inversion of life's story the prison house of the free instincts, consciousness (the most recent and least innate products of the psyche) acts the part of gaoler to the unconscious (the most archaic and least conditioned psychic products). Quite a little coercive State reigns in the psyche, complete even to the Censor. Abominable things are done to the instincts; screams (dreams and obsessions) issue from time to time from the dungeons where the noble bourgeois revolutionaries are being tortured by the authorities. It is a picture in the best anarchist style, with the instincts resorting even to terrorism when necessary, and this terrorism is very sympathetically treated by its historians.

And yet this is untrue. It is in the process of living, in experience, that the instincts, those blind patterns, are modified by reality and, becoming conscious of its necessity, change it and themselves, and so become more free. This embrace with reality is in man mediated by the social environment. That the environment does wrongs to man's mind to-day none will deny. These wrongs are not done because consciousness imprisons the instincts with the fetters of necessity; but because bourgeois man is unconscious of the determinism of his culture. Because of this the instincts are losing such freedom as they attained, are becoming crippled, and less free. Unconsciousness and inexperience, not consciousness and experience, are the gaolers of modern bourgeois man.

2

Thus bourgeois culture cannot use even those good things which it produces. In the ideological sphere as well as the economic, it is embarrassed because it cannot consume the empirical discoveries it has made. Freud, Jung, Adler, McDougall, Kohler, Koffka, Watson, Head, Sherrington, Parsons and MacCurdy have all made discoveries of vital importance for the understanding of mental phenomena, but their full value is lost in the welter of bourgeois culture.

The closed, unplanned worlds of bourgeois science must be broken down, if science is once again to be coherent and fruitful. That is the task of communist science, of dialectical materialism.

Consciousness is a function of life, and we know it primarily as a function of the nervous system. Yet until we see that its relations are not intrinsically peculiar to the nervous system or even to the body as such, but contain elements common to all real matter, though these elements have been carefully rubbed out of the 'matter' of bourgeois physics, we can never escape from mentalism or mechanical materialism. The very nomenclature of modern psychology is mythological.

What is the organ of consciousness? It would be almost reasonable to ask of the earth, what is the organ of liquidity. The answer 'water' would not be very helpful. And yet neurology has an answer of sorts.

The optic thalamus and its outgrowths lie buried in those cerebral hemispheres whose convoluted folds of grey matter, known as the cortex, are hypertrophied in man. The properties of the thalamus have been investigated at a more recent date than those of the cortex. It represents the more primitive portion of man's brain, found well developed even in lower animals. The elaborate cortex is a rich outgrowth of this part of the brain. Naturally therefore the thalamus is regarded as the seat of man's more primitive mental functions, and the cortex of his characteristically human mentation, notably 'reason', 'intelligence', and 'consciousness'.

The thalamus appears to be the grand shunting station for cerebral messages. All sensory relations between brain and objects, save those for smell, are 'projected' in the thalamus and then sent up to be re-projected in the cortex. Smell, however passes straight through to the cortex. Motor messages to nerve plates in muscles, also pass from the motor area of the cortex, down through the thalamus, to be distributed via the spinal cord to the body.*

The cortex consists of fold upon fold of only slightly-differentiated neurones. Its hypertrophy in man is generally correlated with the plasticity of man's behaviour. He comes into the world a *tabula rasa* for habits. Unlike the fixed instinctive reactions of the insects, his behaviour is mainly acquired. It is assumed therefore that the staggeringly complex nerve mesh of the cortex, with its hundreds of millions of cells, is the blank page on which life writes its message.

This has been borne out by the study of cortical lesions. The motor habits of speech, the senses of sight and hearing, the habits of word recognition, writing, and of moving various parts of the body, have all been localised in parts of the cortex.

The primitive nature of the thalamus is suggested by comparison with animals. As one ascends in time the evolutionary tree the cortex grows in bulk, whilst the thalamus

* Motor impulses do not actually pass through the thalamus as this passage might imply. The main motor tract passes between the thalamus and the basal ganglia. The thalamus however has connections with other, more primitive, motor nuclei.—B. H. K.

and its associations do not. Some claim that those have even diminished. It is a matter of terminology. The thalamus itself has perhaps dwindled slightly, but its associated non-cortical outgrowths, which may be assumed to share thalamic functions, have somewhat increased. There is no dispute about the quite disproportionate increase in cortical volume.

However, the argument from morphology might be faulty. The thalamus might after all be like the cortex in function. The experiments of Head, Rivers, Sherrington, and Parsons, have discovered evidence which supports the morphological argument. Where for any reason connections between the thalamus and cortex are severed, so that the cortex is out of action, activity seems to become more instinctive. Up to a point nothing happens, and then there is a sudden and violent reaction, accompanied by emotions of disproportionate strength. This kind of action has been taken to be characteristic of instinct—the 'all or none' reaction—and hence this is held to confirm the primitive character of the thalamus.

Head's bold experiment of severing a nerve in his arm and noting the return of sensation as it healed, uncovered still more interesting phenomena. The experiment led him to differentiate between two forms of sensation, *protopathic* (or primitive) and *epicritic* (or advanced). As the nerve healed protopathic sensation first appeared; then epicritic developed, repressing the older form. One does not develop into the other: there is a dialectic 'jump'.

Protopathic sensation was discovered to have a high threshold. It was difficult to locate. When, for example in the case of pressure, the high threshold was passed, quite suddenly there was a sensation of acute discomfort, but with very poor discrimination or localisation. This 'hit and miss' character of protopathic sensation, as of a man in a rage swiping blindly at some unknown danger, had already been found to be characteristic of thalamic function. Hence Head and his followers connect protopathic or primitive sensation with the thalamus, as representing a primitive form of sensation, repressed by the evolution of the epicritic system.

The epicritic system by contrast is more discriminating, has a low threshold and does not suddenly pass into acute discomfort. This is normal sensation as we experience it.

It is therefore assumed that the cortex is part of the epicritic system, and contrasts with the thalamus. It is discriminating; it does not act rashly, in gusts, but according to the situation. In Head's view it is continually repressing the instinctive activities of the thalamus, by cortical 'back-stroke', and we may equate this cortical control, it is suggested, with that rational consciousness we feel controlling our actions in actual life.

The epicritic sensations are primarily exteroceptive—as for example sight and hearing. The proprioceptive sensations may however be protopathic. As is well known, the internal organs, bones, etc., are not sensitive; we cannot feel our stomach or intestines move in peristalsis. Nonetheless when a certain threshold is passed internally, we experience a sudden agonising pain and a sensation of 'structural discomfort', dull, heavy, and alarming. This kind of sensation, as Head had already found, is characteristic of the protopathic system before the epicritic sensation has manifested itself. Presumably therefore internal sensation is still largely thalamic. Again, when we are 'thrown off our balance' by sudden gusts of rage, it is to be assumed that cortical control has vanished temporarily and our behaviour is thalamic.

This dualism was not accepted without opposition. It was

for instance criticised by neurologists of the standing of Pizron. Nonetheless the general trend of research has if anything confirmed Head's distinction between cortex and thalamus, although the sharpness of many of his definitions has been modified. As a result it is usual to schematise the neurological basis of consciousness as follows: All sensation comes *via* the nerve receptors to the thalamus, where it would provoke instinctive 'all-or-none' reaction, were it not for cortical control. It then passes on to the cortex, where it emerges as conscious perception. Discriminative motor habits arising out of this perception are assumed to be lodged in the cortex, while the more instinctive motorisms are located in the thalamus. Thus the general view is that consciousness is primarily, if not solely, the activation of sensation or motor traces in the cortex, and that all delicate affective shades are similarly cortical. Thalamic activity, it is assumed, is associated with unconscious or subliminal perceptions and instinctive motorisms. All violent effective outbursts, particularly severe pains, are assumed to be thalamic. The thalamus is the rebel, the seat of the unconscious, the instinctive proletariat, which that well-educated and refined bureaucracy, the cortex, with its unemotional logical consciousness, keeps (not without difficulty) in order.

At a still lower level is the bulbo-spinal system, concerned with simple reflexes. This may be omitted from our discussion for the moment.

Certain psychologists, such as Marston, have suggested that consciousness is primarily a function of the synapses. This however will not affect the present argument. Since wherever there is a nerve connection there is a synapse, and since no one suggested all synapses are simultaneously active, the synaptic theory leaves it open as to which parts of the nervous system are in fact concerned in consciousness.

In any case there are more synapses in the cortex than elsewhere. Therefore it is fair to say that the view we have outlined represents the trend of opinion, as far as there can be such a thing, amongst modern neurologists. It will be seen that it is still influenced by bourgeois biology. The free instincts are controlled by the cortex. Experience throttles unconscious life. Freedom is the unconsciousness of the necessity of reality, learned in experience.

It would however be just as accurate to picture the thalamus as the organ of conscious instinct and the cortex as the organ of unconscious thought. In either case we are simply playing about with terms. Consciousness is not so simple as that.

Cortical consciousness is equated in current neurological theory with epicritic sensation. The essence of epicritic sensation is fine discrimination. Thalamic sensation—which is *un*conscious or (as Rivers visualises it) repressed by cortical control—is lacking in discrimination. Thus a light touch on the skin, easily detected by the epicritic system, has to be increased to a hard pressure before it is perceived by the protopathic system, which then explodes affectively.

How does this theory square with the facts of consciousness?

Few of the docrines of psychology receive more general assent than that of subliminal impressions. Impressions have to reach a certain threshold value before they are consciously perceived. That such impressions, although not perceived consciously, have yet left memory traces, *i.e.* have been perceived unconsciously, is evidenced by the fact that they can be recovered in hypnotic trance, when what is loosely called 'the unconscious' is made accessible. The phenomena of hyperæsthesia are explained in this way. Sounds, scents and cutaneous and visual discriminations not normally in the conscious field, are made accessible by the inclusion with the ego in hypnotic trance of a large part of what is normally unconscious sensation. In the same way slight impressions, separately unconscious, appear eventually by repetition to summate until they can rise above the threshold of consciousness, when the ego then becomes 'aware' of the previous repetitions.

Now this at once raises the query, damaging for the usual theory, why consciousness should show all the characteristics of protopathic sensation—restricted field and lack of fine discrimination—while unconsciousness proves itself endowed with epicritic discrimination and range of sensation. Head's view, as we have said, is that epicritic sensation 'repressed' protopathic sensation, or made it unconscious. The facts concerning subliminal impressions, if valid, contradict it. They do not however prove the reverse, for Head's own experiments show that protopathic sensation can also be conscious. The conclusion would appear to be that consciousness has nothing to do with either epicritic or protopathic sensation, nor repression with unconsciousness, but that we must think along other lines in order to understand what the relations are.

Let us consider such a simple question as the ordinary visual field, and its connection with degrees of consciousness. It is well known that we do not regard the visual field as an undifferentiated whole, but that different parts of it have different values. This is expressed in the older theory of a faculty of 'attention' (which, like consciousness, has been located in the cortex) and in the *gestalt* or 'field' theory, which is really an elaborate attention psychology made objective. Thus motion of objects attracts the attention to them. We see *interesting* objects. A woman sees a bat; an artist's attention is caught by features of light and shade unnoticed to others; a detective sees a criminal face. We all tend to see shapes in shadows, figures in clouds, to fill out and round off contrasts, according to the schemes made clear by gestalt experiments. Attention is a name for the actual element in perception.

Now though we may say that all the visual field is 'consciousness', it is plain that different degrees of consciousness range over the visual field. Thus the sportsman, watching rabbits, sees a vague background with a very distinct brown animal moving over it. Perceptually the rabbit is more conscious to him than its surroundings, and more discrimination is made as to size, markings of coat, and movements in this rabbit. A botanist surveying the same scene might however see nothing clearly except a flower in the field.

Here is made plain the nature of the contradiction between epicritic and protopathic sensations and consciousness. Consciousness is at its highest point in the rabbit region of the visual field to the sportsman. Even the beast's whiskers are clear to his eye. Here sensation is epicritic.

At the same time, in the rest of the visual field nothing is consciously noted but a green blur. Here then sensation is protopathic. But in both cases sensation is conscious. The weaker conscious sensation is protopathic, the stronger epicritic. If, however, the sportsman were to be hypnotised, our knowledge of subliminal perception compels us to believe that we could recover, out of that green blur, details of perception which the sportsman had not consciously experienced. Thus here sensation, *unconscious* sensation, is epicritic. Experiments with eidetic imagery seem to confirm this view.

This compels us to suppose that consciousness, in its vividness or degree or even actual existence, cannot be correlated with either epicritic or protopathic sensation. It can however be correlated with what has come to be called interest or 'attention'. Interest is an affective phenomenon. Consciousness therefore is affective tone.

To return to another feature of the cortex—the richness and plasticity of its reactions. Man's thought is almost certainly more rich and plastic than that of any animal. His range of memories, the subtlety of his discrimination among them and his faculty of language with all the richness of content it involves, are outcomes of this. Consequently we rightly regard the hypertrophied human cortex as the seat of this peculiarly human richness of association and mental structure.

But when we come to consciousness, we find in it a feature which is peculiarly uncortical—its thinness and *linear* character. Consciousness is a one-track activity. Man can normally only follow one train of thought at a time, and this train consists, even in the richest thinkers, of a succession of single images in the spotlight of consciousness, surrounded by a dim, half-conscious fuzz. None of the richness characteristic of human thought in the universal, is characteristic of consciousness in the particular. Everyone knows we can only concentrate on one thing at a time. Moreover the intimacy of the connection is shown by the kind of inverse law it follows. The more conscious and vivid the mental product, the more linear and sparse its real content. It does not seem poor to us, because of its vividness. The height of its consciousness seems to atone for its simplicity; but still it is simple. The thing that 'worries' us and demands all our attention, obliterates all other associations. The sight of one we love makes us 'forget everything else'. The approach of a mad bull blots out the rest of the visual field.

But this is very uncortical, for the cortex is by hypothesis the seat of immensely complex motor kinæsthetic and sensory co-ordinations. Consciousness appears unable to use more than a few of these at a time; and the richer it is, the fewer they are. If we regard the human cortex, in a well-educated person, as consisting of *n* potentialities, consciousness at any moment can only be concerned with a minute fraction of *n*. The rest are unconscious. Therefore the cortex is primarily an unconscious rather than a conscious organ. It is like a library of knowledge with only one owner. Despite its immense resources, the owner at any one instant can only scan one word in one line in one book, though given time and opportunity he can read what he likes and find what he likes in the realm of human knowledge.

Therefore, cortical consciousness is really chiefly cortical unconsciousness. The cortex is the great unopened dictionary, the grand reservoir of the temporarily forgotten. Consciousness in the cortex is the glowing of a few neurones out of hundreds of millions—an exception, a tiny localisation. Unless we think the unconscious of no importance, we would do better to regard the cortex as the seat of unconsciousness. This would give man a larger unconscious than the beasts, but is not this just what we would expect—is not the beast's knowledge more at its instant command, less influenced by memory and association and therefore by the temporarily forgotten but recallable? True, though forgotten it is recallable, but no one would restrict the name 'unconscious' to the completely unavailable, for, if it is completely unavailable, by no means can it be proved to exist. We make therefore the suggestion that unconsciousness and not consciousness, is the distinctive feature of man's cortical outgrowth; and that this shows the weakness of current distinctions between consciousness and unconsciousness.

* * * * *

These considerations suggest others. What governs the tiny localisation of conscious light in the vast Arctic night of the cortex? The feature of the cortex, histologically, is its lack of differentiation. Each part is like any other part. The localisations of speech and similar functions seem arbitrary. How much more arbitrary seems the local play of consciousness.

What this suggests can be shown by analogy. In a network of electrified wires we see, constant at one point, a glowing 'hot spot'. We might suppose either that this was due to a blowpipe flame from outside, applied to that spot, or to a kind of local short due to the connections of the wires.

If, however, we saw that the hot spot moved continually about from wire to wire, we should infer, on the normal principle of induction, that there was some mobile outside cause. Either the blowpipe flame was being moved, or there was some switching apparatus continually changing the direction of the current. In either case, though the hot spot was in the wire system, we should regard it as external.

In the same way, considering the moving spotlight of consciousness in the cortical library, it seems that we must regard its movement as due to some other cause, some external switchboard. We have already correlated consciousness, both in existence and vividness, with affective tone. Assuming that the thalamus is primarily concerned in affective activity, the switching organ, directing consciousness into the local cortical channel, must be thalamic. If therefore anything has the right to be called the organ of consciousness, it would be the thalamus. But this again shows the inadequate conception of consciousness current in psychology. A conscious thought is the affective 'heating' of a cortical trace. The greater the heat, the greater the consciousness. The cortical trace is not the consciousness, because the cortex is, by assumption, an enormous mass of traces, all undifferentiated and all unconscious. The consciousness, if we must make a mere quality substantive, is the affective heat, for that and that alone produces consciousness. But actually to separate affect and idea is Aristotelean; it is like separating form and matter.

Our theory has certain analogies with the kinetic theory of heat. The molecules correspond to the cortex. The vibration of the molecules *is* the consciousness. The perpetually boiling organ, selectively communicating its vibrations, is the thalamus. Its boiling is a reflection of the whole relation between body and environment.

Since the organism is a unity, consciousness must be unitary in nature, and the more intense the vividness, the greater the limitation of consciousness. It is wrong, however, to equate this with a constant supply of conscious energy, which must therefore be either deep and thin or wide and shallow.

The reason for the limitations of content when vividness is present must be sought elsewhere. Attention to externals, *i.e.* to objects in the visual or stimulus field, is characteristic of all animals. It is simply that activity which is regarded as characteristic of life. Sensibility is a readiness to respond to certain stimuli, which in itself implies activity towards such stimuli. Simple organisms respond to food particles in the tactile field; higher animals to prey or mates or traces suggestive of them in the visual field. Men notice a wider range of 'things' and discriminate more subtly, but always the vivid conscious part of the visual field is something that can awake their instincts, which in turn are defined as the entities which are awakened by those particular stimuli.

Thus consciousness is simply a specific feature of sensibility, a form of behaviour. Sensibility involves on the one hand an innate response to certain things and, on the other hand, certain things in the environment to be interested in. For example, in a unicellular organism, sensibility involves the tendency to be irritated by contact with small round objects (potential food) and also the small round objects at any given moment in contact with the organism.

This stimulus elicits the response, and there is no gulf, only a matter of degree, between this simple manifestation of irritability, and the sportsman with a tendency to be irritated by the rabbit and the presence of the rabbit in his visual field, both making up the consciousness of the rabbit in all its vividness.

True he is also conscious of the green blur which is the rest of the visual field. But if an organism is to be highly irritated by all small round objects that are food, like the amœba, it must be slightly irritated, as the amœba is, by all small round objects tactually presented. In the same way, if the animal or the sportsman is to be irritated by the presence of prey in the visual field, if he is to 'notice' them, he must be slightly irritated by the visual field as a whole and always must be slightly conscious of it. In other words, before we can become conscious of a thing, we must first become unconscious of it. We must have awareness over a wide general field.

It might be thought that the visual field, in its all inclusiveness, cannot be compared with an amœba in tactile contact with a hard object. But in fact, the visual field is an empirical and exclusive construction. It neglects most of the possible wave-lengths of radiation, ignores distant features, and does not observe any molecular or atomic phenomena or real movements above and below a certain speed. It is in fact as much a concentration of interest as a protozoan's exclusive concern with small round objects. The protozoan's whole world is small round objects. Our visual field is similarly limited to phenomena which, as we evolved, have proved of interest to us, such as the common light octave (in colour).

An instinct is an innate response of a certain nature to external or somatic stimuli, or both. We should not consider an animal as possessing instincts but only potential instincts, just as the cortex as a whole is not conscious but only potentially conscious. We should regard instinct only as it appears in behaviour, as a response to some situation. It is true that we should thus never get a pure instinct, for the situation is always slightly different and therefore even in insects the behaviour is always slightly different. This is all to the good.

This would simplify the theory of mentation. Living response or sensibility, including conscious mentation, consists of potential instinct, which is the whole sum of inborn responses to somatic stimuli or environmental stimuli. This is a purely fictive conception, but methodologically useful, like the 'genotype' in heredity. Actually nothing is ever known, either in behaviour or in consciousness, except potential instinct reacting to its somatic or environmental stimuli and being changed thereby. Where we part company with the behaviourist, who does not recognise consciousness, is that we recognise consciousness and include it as a form of behaviour. Thus we regard the visual field as instinctive behaviour modified by experience. It is the instinctive response of the cortical and thalamic projective areas to stimuli. The stimuli are to us so complex in the normal visual field that we naively regard them as 'all reality', instead of just a selection from it. This brings conscious perception within the field of causality. It determines and is determined, and this we already know from quantum physics. Observation is an active process—a return to Cartesian theories of vision on a higher plane.

Instincts are modified in experience. Some, like those of the insects, are only slightly modifiable. Others, like the dog's food response or man's various responses to stimuli, are capable of far more conditioning. This can be regarded as an enriching or complicating of them. Thus the instinctive visual field of the baby is modified, and made richer and more discriminating, in the grown man. Innate behaviour becomes in experience complex behaviour. This is a simple dialectic law of development.

The visual field is a conditioned, instinctive response to stimuli. There is a slight response to a large number of stimuli, which we may call simply vision. This slight sensory response guarantees the visual, aural or tactual field as a whole. Under the influence of some more specialised innate response—to prey, mates or danger—we notice more eagerly, more consciously and more vividly some one object in that visual, aural, or tactile field. We behave towards it in a different way. The greater specificity of the response makes us consider a unit instinct is at work, but this is only a name for a consistent difference in behaviour towards a class of objects. It is thus determined also by the environment.

The linear nature of consciousness, limited in proportion to its vividness, is therefore necessary. Instinct is action. The efficiency of the body and its very survival can only be secured by the fact that it acts integrally. The higher the organism, the more true we find this integration of response, a unity in diversity. Since consciousness is part of the complete response, it must be all of a piece with the rest of the response, including the body's overt action. This means we must only see or think of those things most immediately relevant to the instinctive action as a whole. Thus the tendency of the organism to flee from danger ensures that, when danger appears in the visual field, the organism is not conscious of its tailor's unpaid bill, what it ate for dinner last week, or the infinity of the Universe, but only of the mad bull, and the nearest exit from the field, while at the same time the body's response is limited to visceral vaso-motor constriction, emission of adrenalin into the blood from the suprarenal glands, and rapid running movement with the legs.

Plainly the ego, insofar as we regard it as the stream of consciousness, is our name for this fact. The integrity of the organism creates the ego, not the ego the organism.

The association of affects or emotions with the instincts has always been puzzling. The 'instincts' seem to give rise to affects, and yet instinctive activity can appear without them. Restricting ourself to the case of conscious perception of a dangerous object in the visual field, we see that there are two elements in the response—intra-somatic behaviour (adrenalic secretion and so forth)—and extra-somatic (running). The first assists the second, Vision is only involved as a part of action, and is stripped of all but its bare essentials for the purpose. Therefore the simpler the extra-somatic response, the more 'one-to-one' its correspondence with innate reflexes, the less the need for the activation of the cortical traces of experience. Both affect and consciousness are therefore functions of the complexity of the potentially stimulating field, and its relation to the modified reflexes of the organism.

Certain animals, for example the insects, in spite of elaborate instinctive activity, are closely geared to an unvarying chain. The sphex will sting only one species of wasp, and only in a certain way. There is therefore in spite of the complexity of the overt behaviour, a poverty of alternative objects and a poverty of alternative behaviour. The correspondence is virtually one-to-one. We should expect such creatures to experience no affects and no consciousness. Stimuli and reflexes match perfectly and weave an almost unvarying fabric.

Nonetheless we must regard consciousness as a matter of

degree. Just as heat and cold are simply varying rates of molecular motion, which we divide subjectively into 'hotter than ours.' and 'colder than ours.' consciousness and unconsciousness simply represent degrees of affective vividness. Many states subliminal for us might well be blinding consciousness for fishes. Even in insects there cannot be anything like perfect one-to-one correspondence of innate instinct to stimulus. There is no absolute degree of consciousness. It is the ego that is conscious but the ego in turn is composed of a series of experiences selected above a certain indistinct threshold. Naturally, to this ego anything below the threshold seems unconscious, but this is merely because it is the ego which is doing the description.

* * * * *

The conception of a switchboard is often used for neural operations. It seems less objectionable than most analogies, for the neurone undoubtedly has junctions, and transmits impulses along its length by means of waves of potential difference. But it differs from a switchboard in having no operator, a fact which causes psychologists to invent instincts, consciousnesses, and egos which operate the switches. Perhaps the automatic telephone may eliminate these mythical deities. The brain is an extremely elaborate automatic telephone system. in which the stimuli are the subscribers dialling, in which the apparatus is modified by experience, and in which the body is part of the system—flesh, blood and all.

In all switchboard schematisations of the neural system, the cortex is pictured as the seat of a highly competent Postmaster-General, directing all the other chains of relays, down to the humble reflexes in the basement. This P.M.G. is usually equated with consciousness. Our hypothesis has no use for this overworked official.

If we must personify, let us personify the thalamus, and let us imagine it, at a primitive level, faced with the task of making more epicritic its sensations, and its action more discriminating. It will do so by manufacturing an intricate system through which sensations and motor activities can be relayed, sorted out, stored and recombined, and where the increased complexity of the possible combinations will make more epicritic the actions. In other words, the cortex (if we must personify) is the *servant* of the thalamus rather than the master. (But either picture is inaccurate.)

Any engineer faced with the task of increasing the possible combinations of a given circuit—*e.g.* the number of telephone numbers diallable—would at once see that some 'hierarchy' must be called for. A must control B and C; in turn B will control D and E and C will control G and F, and so on. Only in this way can unity of action as well as discrimination, be secured. Yet it is just unity which is the feature of consciousness, represented in the ego and its linear form of thought. Hence for the arbiter or controller of cortical activity, we must look to some concentrated organ holding all the cortical threads in its hands. This would be, for sheer mechanical reasons, the optic thalamus.

Consciousness streams on with different contents, yet we feel there is an unchanging basis for it, sharing all experiences alike. This unchanging basis, this ego, is something that has access to vast stores of experience, but itself maintains its general pattern. This would correspond to the thalamus, through which all active ingoing and outgoing impulses pass, but which has itself little mnemic grey matter. The cortex on the other hand is highly mnemic.

Let it be understood that we do not regard consciousness as exclusively thalamic, or the ego as seated in the thalamus and its outgrowths. This is to make the mistake of the mythologists. The thalamus, because of its strategic position, is the spear-point of consciousness. Consciousness is a behaviour of the whole nervous system. It is one out of a number of conditioned responses to stimuli.

Inhibition is a feature of consciousness but is not peculiar to it. The amœba performs, in response to a given stimulus, one out of several possible actions. The others therefore are inhibited. The organism which runs in response to danger inhibits other possible actions. The organism which thinks is innervating certain neurone groups, corresponding to older motor and sensory groupings, and this constitutes a thought or wish or feeling, one out of many possible, the others being inhibited or unconscious.

Consider a definite situation: *There is a bull in the field of vision.* This stimulus, as a result of thalamic switching, activates adrenal and visceral innervations, and produces a general somatic readiness to make the fear-response. Owing to the nature of the situation—the choice of flight or fighting, and the different paths available for both—there is a good deal of thalamic sparking among different possible muscular reactions, and these thalamic sparkings correspond to fear-consciousness. Some of the energy as a result of more thalamic switching flows into the cortex, where it innervates nerve groups corresponding to thoughts of danger, possible paths, and vague remorse at having taken the wrong short-cut—all glowing with the fear affect. No fear affect, no consciousness of these thoughts.

Thus the conscious field consists of protopathic visceral circuits, a mediating thalamic circuit, and an epicritic cortical circuit. We cannot say that consciousness is located exclusively in any one of these circuits. True, no one is conscious without a cortex, but neither are they conscious without a thalamus. All are concerned; all are integrated in the one response to the stimulus; all combine to produce the one conscious field.

In this pressing danger, we might examine the bull more closely. We then draw on the traces in the cortical retinal area, to discriminate more closely the features of the bull. Could it be pacified? Is it a large one? Could we side-step its charge? This more discriminating perception, in which memory enters, is the thalamus drawing on the cortex for information, or if we like it is affectivity piling up and leaking into other cortical areas.

We may visualise the bulbo-spinal area as the home of innate reflexes which experience will not greatly change. The cortex on the other hand is the place where all motor and sensory experiences leave traces, which because of their elaborate wiring, will be more discriminating, more easily split up and more plastic and learnable than elsewhere. Moreover since their knowledge will be required when instinct has not a one-to-one correlation between stimulus and response, it is precisely the cortical cells which will receive the affective glow of a 'puzzled' thalamus sparking and trying various alternative lines. This emotion will therefore be always associated with cortical contents, except in severe pains or thalamic protopathic explosions. Hence our mistaken belief that it is a matter of cortical 'control'.

Rather is it a matter of cortical advice. The thalamus might plead that it is only 'human' and cannot remember everything, and neurologists would admit that its deficiency in grey matter would explain its poor memory. Nevertheless, as a result of æons of experience, with comparatively little differentiation, it is a magnate of strong will and simple notions. It has the main policy of the firm at its finger tips. Such persons are normally put at the helm of power. At its service, however, it has a staff of experts, and in any ordinary circumstance it consults them (thought). Naturally, in view of their experience, it acts on their advice. The body of experts might therefore claim that they control their chief. Nonetheless the reality of thalamic power is shown in all emergencies calling for instantaneous motor response of a nature so simple that the thalamus has known it for centuries. The cortex is ignored. Again, if a complex situation recurs, even the thalamic memory is sufficient to deal with the situation. This is habit.*

Consciousness might be regarded as an affective light, which plays upon cortical, thalamic, visceral and sensory neurones.† They 'clump' together and separate out. Hence our elaborate classifications of conscious affects, feelings, thoughts, memories and percepts—all purely bogus, if we regard them as describing separate entities. Naturally a cortical neurone, under affective activity, 'feels' different to a visceral or sensory neurone, because it has a different chronaxy, composition, architecture and mnemic past, but its feeling is pooled in the common structure.

If Marston is right, and consciousness is a synaptic phenomenon, this would account for the variation of affectivity. A simple reflex would not be conscious, because the synapses are firmly 'closed'. When however they are open there is a sparking, which is an affect and goes to compose consciousness. In protopathic systems a heavy stimulus would be needed to open the somewhat 'rusty' synapses, but the spark would be correspondingly intense and

* There is no evidence to support the view that an habitual response to a complex situation is dependent on 'thalamic memory'. Rather would the work of Pavlov's school and recent experience of head injuries suggest that an intact cortex is essential for this type of response. By contrast with the emergency situation described above however such a familiar situation will evoke a response with a minimum of affect and consciousness—*i.e.* be another example of the role of the cortex as the organ of unconsciousness.—B. H. K.

† Cortical, thalamic, visceral and sensory neurones. The meaning of the passage is obscured by this classification, since sensory neurones are both thalamic and cortical, and visceral are mainly thalamic. What is clearly intended however is a contrast between the cells of the cortex and those of the evolutionarily older parts of the brain, including the thalamus.—B. H. K.

explosive. The smooth 'frictionless' synapses of the cortex and epicritic sensory system open and close quietly. The cortex appears to control and modify response as a whole, because it forms a part of most circuits. It corresponds to a capacitance effect in radio. There is no 'seat' of integration in an organism. Integration, precisely because it is integration, is the function of the entire organism.

Directed thinking is an affective river in the cortex. All thinking has a strong affective component, otherwise it would not be conscious. Why (to take apparently the least affective instance) do we turn over one of thousands of possible mathematical problems? Because that one interests us. Interest is nothing but affect.

The affective association of conscious ideas, rediscovered by Freud and Janet, is not therefore odd, but the only possible law of conscious thought considered subjectively. Affects are the stuff of ideas. Association by contiguity is meaningless neurologically. It explains association of ideas by another idea, that of contiguity. Needless to say ideas whose original stimuli are spatio-temporally contiguous, are likely to share the same affective tone, and as such are likely to revive together. Given in every experience is a subject and object. Association by contiguity is objective association of experiences.

Whether it is the cat springing precisely on its prey, or the mathematician solving a problem, the behaviour is the same in principle. First there is the tendency called forth by the stimulus—the desire to solve the problem. Then the conformity of the behaviour with reality, that is the flowing of the affective current of interest, by elaborate and tortuous synaptic paths, among just those cortical cells which experience has shown to be necessary. The animal stalking its prey, fatigued and stung by the brushwood, and the mathematician, with wrinkled brow, solving the thorny problem, are both exhibiting the same behaviour, except that the animal's is overt, the mathematician's intra-somatic. The exultant pounce of the animal, fatigue forgotten, and the joyful 'Eureka!' of the mathematician, his frown changing to a smile, are evidences of similar terminations to the transaction.

Sleep frees us from attention to present reality. It inhibits by closing the sensory roads (a patient with anæsthesia of the skin is liable to fall asleep at any moment). Since the cortex is the great storehouse of memory, *i.e.* of recent reality, it is asleep. We never smell in dreams,* and smell alone of the senses goes to the cortex without thalamic intervention. In sleep, the 'instinct', or 'innate tendency' to conform to reality, which is simply the connection of the cortex to the nervous circuit, is cut off. Our learning is forgotten. We mould our thoughts like a child. The thalamus reveals that, without his advisers, he is in spite of his energy a savage. The strongly visual character of dreams is presumably due to the large retinal projection on the thalamus.† The fact that most dream contents can be referred to the previous day, might be attributed to the unmnemic character of the thalamus. There may be some cortical activity in dream, but the primitive protopathic character of dream sensations, the indistinct faces, the condensation of images—which would be characteristic of a non-discriminating organ—all

* Smell in dreams. This statement is controversial but if incorrect does not vitiate the main argument, since the rhinopallium, or part of the cortex which deals with smell, is much more akin to the thalamus than other parts of the cortex.

† Thalamus and vision. The thalamus was at one time known as the optic thalamus, a misnomer since the fibres of the optic tract do not relay in the thalamus. There are however other relay stations in the optic apparatus which may play a similar role in regard to visual stimuli. It is obvious that dreams are not wholly explicable on the basis of thalamic activity and that a cortical element must be assumed. The general argument, that in the dream state the role of the thalamus is dominant, can however be supported.—B. H. K.

seem thalamic. Since we have not equated consciousness with the cortex, the vividness and reality of dreams present no difficulty. Dreams are the opposite to '*déjà vue*' phenomena, in which real percepts seem memories. In dream, memories seem real percepts. The former some psychiatrists attribute to thalamic inactivity; the latter therefore we attribute to thalamic activity. By active and inactive, we mean active and inactive relatively to the cortex.

Now all this is very well as far as it goes. We have tried to join the two ends of mental and biological psychology. But we reach a certain point with neurology, and then are up against the difficulty that neurology is a branch of biology, that outside stands the closed world of bourgeois physics, and, arbitrarily planted on top of the closed world of neurology, is the closed world of mentalism, or bourgeois faculty psychology. By the very definitions of bourgeois psychology, we are forced to regard innervations and thoughts, nerves and consciousness, matter and mind as distinct classes of entities, mutually exclusive. Until dialectical materialism has broken down this exclusiveness, not only in psychology but in physics, biology, philosophy and sociology, how can we begin to formulate a theory of consciousness that will not be dualistic and strained?

But we can perhaps indicate the road, starting from the foundations. We must sweep away the concept of the bourgeois in opposition to and separate from the environment.

In this Newtonian schematisation, the bourgeois and the environment obey entirely different laws; the bourgeois stops at his skin. The consciousness is 'something' that sits inside, while outside 'reality' raps on the nerve-endings in code, which code is 'interpreted' inside the skin. This is precisely how Eddington formulates the situation, evidently believing it to be the 'scientific' view.

But in fact the bourgeois is only an organised whirlpool

of matter in his environment, constantly changing, constantly being renewed. The consciousness is the organisation of a part of it, but the organisation is not separate from the matter, like a concept or universal. The matter is organised. The organisation is a quality of matter.

The Universe becomes. Not merely man becomes, but change, motion and development are the law of the Universe. The Universe does not change and become in Time. Relativity and quantum physics clearly show that time *is* the change, and the becoming. All phenomena A, B, and C, etc. are connected so that A is included in B, B in C, C in D, and so on. This inclusion in difference is Becoming, development, and reality. This involves a substratum of likeness in the Universe, that which changes, that which is the same in all change. This we abstract as space, as the aspects of matter expressed in the conservation laws (mass, energy, interval, action). This we regard as the stuff of the Universe. This is what mathematics is concerned with, what quantity is, what the basis is of all predictive laws of science.

But equally it involves a superstructure of unlikeness in the Universe—the change as change, the difference in all events. This we abstract as Time, as the qualities in matter not obeying conservation laws (colour, consciousness, beauty). This we regard as the *aspect* of the Universe, precisely because it is the difference that interests us. This is quality, the basis of all art and sensuous culture.

But any absolute dichotomy into reality and appearance, space and time, matter and motion, primary and secondary qualities or object and subject, is erroneous and denies the reality either of change or of existence. Both are intimately blended in becoming. It is not separate things that become entirely in themselves, but the Universe is one, there are determining relations between all phenomena. These determining relations are the becoming. If any group were self-determined, it would be unknowable and unknowing in its relations to the rest, and would not therefore exist. The Universe is a material unity.*

This is true, not merely of life but of all that is, from consciousness to physics, and this guarantees that these worlds cannot in fact be closed nor their laws remain unchanged. And change, the increase in organisation, is newness; it is what consciousness is. But we can never set something aside, and say: This is entirely new, it has no old in it—for that would be to *separate* something from the Universe, to deny change and dichotomise becoming.

The like, that which remains is, in the biological sphere, instinct and habit and heredity. The unlike, that which is new, is experience, knowledge and acquired characters. Each generates the other in dialectic movement. In the evolution of consciousness, instinct is experience, gives rise to memory and affect, and is now no longer the old instinct. We may lodge experience in the cortex and instinct in the bulbo-spinal system, but both can only be separated in abstraction. There is only bodily behaviour, that is, material becoming in which body and environment are involved.

Body and environment are in constant determining relations. Perception is not the decoding of tappings on the skin. It is a determining relation between neural and environmental electrons. Every part of the body not only affects the other parts but is also in determining relations with the rest of reality. It is determined by it and determines it, this interchange producing development—the constantly changing series of interlocking events, A, B, C . . . Of this multitude of relations, spatio-temporal, perceptual and mnemic, we distinguish a certain group, changing as the world changes, not with it or separately from it but in

* This position is fully stated in the essay *Reality*, see below, p. 210

mutually determining interaction with it. This selection, rich, highly organised and recent, we call the consciousness, or our ego. We do not select it out. In the process of development it separates out, as life separated out, as suns and planets, and the elements separated out from the process of becoming. Separated out, and still changing, it is consciousness, it is *us* in so far as we regard outselves as conscious egos. But in separating out, it does not completely separate out, any more than any element did. It remains, like them in determining relation with the rest of the Universe, and the study of the organisation of this developed structure, of its inner relations and the relations of the system with all other systems in the Universe, is psychology—not bourgeois psychology, but the psychology of dialectical materialism.

We can say that such a psychology will only purge itself of the dualisms and anarchy of present-day psychology by realising that it is the science of the minds of men living in concrete society. These men are material bodies entering into social relations with each other and the rest of the material universe. This means the abandonment of the mythical categories of bourgeois psychology, which has proved itself unable to advance beyond the conception of the abstract individual psyche, the self-consciousness of the individual in civil society—in a society where the individual, because society has not yet found itself, has lost himself.

V

REALITY

A Study in Bourgeois Philosophy

IT has been obvious for some time that the world of physics has been deviating farther and farther from the world of perception. The world of physics is a world composed of points and instants and lines, bare of quality. Nothing in it can be felt, smelt, or seen. The world of relativity physics, which combines space and time, seems to take us ever farther from reality as directly experienced. How is this, for physics is built up from the results of perception? The discrepancy between Newton's and Einstein's theories was settled in favour of Einstein by perception—the Michelson-Morley experiment, the eclipse experiment and observation of Mercury's movements. The perceived world therefore is primary and gives status to the various possible self-consistent logical worlds. The perceived world is *real*. Should it not therefore be possible to express the world of physics in terms of less abstract entities? Could we not make it *sound* like the real world? That was the goal of Whitehead's method of Extensive Abstraction.

To take an example, space may be defined as built up of points, and *betweenness*, a property of these points; and these points may be defined in various ways. The Euclidean method was to define a point as an entity having position but no magnitude, which is obviously a thing never met with in perception. Points may also be defined as the class of ordered triads of real numbers with their signs, which seems an even more remote definition but is, thanks to the development of Cantorian transfinites, one which gives the required properties of continuity to space. Either definition is equally satisfactory for developing a geometry.

Whitehead suggests instead that we should regard points as of the class of 'sets' of volumes. For example, the set of concentric spheres converging in a limit gives all the extensive relations of a point. The intensive properties of such a set are not what we might expect from a point, but the intensive relations of such entities do not concern us any more than the interior of the earth concerns the map-maker. Whitehead develops his theory with great logical skill. He treats time in a similar way, using a class of overlapping events to represent the 'instant' of older physics. Russell has a method different in detail, but similar in principle.

Whitehead and Russell therefore make the curious assumption that 'volumes' or 'events' are more gross, and perceptually obvious to anyone than points or instants. But a volume is an abstract idea. Our sensory surfaces, with which we gain our knowledge of external reality, are all areas, not volumes, and the nerve endings are dotted about this area, each ending providing a point of sensation, which is a kind of minimum sensory datum. Thus sensation is, like mathematical space, built up of points, lines and areas, and these are built up by experience into volumes. Even a line or area will be explored by the motion of the point nerve-endings over it. Points can therefore claim at least as much concrete existence in perception as volumes. True, physiological points, unlike geometrical points, have magnitude, but it does not feel as if they had, because they constitute a threshold. In any case, perceptual volumes differ as widely from geometrical volumes as sensory from geometrical points.

* *V. The Analysis of Matter.*

The perception of abstract volumes in fact require a high order of sophistication. We never perceive abstract volume without considerable education in abstractions. I doubt if anyone even among painters, *saw* volume, until Cézanne. Neither primitive man, nor the Bushman, nor the average child, perceive volume in the abstract, if their paintings are any clue. It is always *stuff*, voluminous things, vapour, clouds, mass, that we perceive. Matter is perceptual; volume is not.

But I am even more critical of the assumption that it is only from what we perceive that physical abstractions are built up. On what grounds can this be justified? It is I who experience. My conscious world is filled, not only with things, volumes, points, but with desires, hopes, and memories. Why must these be omitted? Why do those very philosophers such as Kant, Whitehead and Russell, who hold the egoistic components of the conscious field to be primary, demand that physics be built up out of secondary entities?

They do so because the bourgeois philosopher cannot help producing this dualism, and yet he remains unconscious of its scurce. It is not Berkeley who fights mechanical materialism, but Berkeley who generates it. Condillac does not refute solipsism, he produces it. Hume does not dissolve the causal world of physics in which atoms move according to the foresight of a divine calculator; on the contrary, it is Hume who calls such a parody of reality into existence.

Given in reality is subject and object. No sphere of reality is absolutely self-determined, for if it were it would be unknowable, and therefore would not exist. Between subject and object exists a network of relations, including the *conscious field*. Since no part of reality is isolated, this conscious field must directly or indirectly have determining links with every part of reality. Since reality is becoming. subject to endless change, this conscious field may continually increase in size and still more intricately develop inside reality.

Because it is a relation or sum of relations the conscious field 'contains' (or has as terms) both subject and object, by whose interaction it is generated. Now in the analysis of this field there are four alternatives.

(*a*) We may sort this bunch of relations, each of which has the form s-o (subject related to object), on the assumption that o depends on s, which is self-determined. We then get a world of phenomena in which everything known is generated by the subject or 'I', which is therefore primary. This of course is solipsism.

(*b*) We may sift through all these relations on the assumption that s depends on o, which is self-determined. We then get a world of phenomena in which everything known is generated by the object or 'external' world, which is therefore primary. This is mechanical materialism.

Either point of view lands us in difficulties. If the subject is self-determined, how does it come into existence? If the object is self-determined, how does it come to be known? If all relations (*i.e.* qualities) are not completely real but only one term is real and the other dependent and secondary, what in fact *are* the real parts of qualities? Whether we adopt position (*a*) or (*b*) we reach the depressing conclusion that no qualities are *really* real. If we are physicists, and our programme is to confine ourselves to qualities independent of the subject—objective facts—we soon find that the observer is involved in all such qualities as colour, smell, taste. Further research, such as that of relativity physics, shows us that the observer is even involved in such apparently objective qualities as size, shape, mass, motion, time, distance. In all such qualities the observer must be specified.

We finally get nothing absolute but mathematical equations, which express only the comparability of these qualities among themselves, and are therefore purely metrical. But mathematical equations are thoughts; they do not exist concretely. We are therefore back at a completely subjective world, having started out in pursuit of a completely objective world.

(*b*) If we are philosophers, instead of physicists, and our programme is to confine ourselves to qualities independent of the object—the *general* truths achievable by 'pure' thought—we soon find that the object is involved in all such apparenty subjective qualities as causality, perception, thought. We finally get nothing absolute but Universals, or concepts such as Whiteness, Truth, and the like. These concepts must however exist independently of the thinker's brain, for this brain is a particular object. These Universals must one by one be stripped of all the distinctions that arise from particularities, and thus we are left with nothing but the laws of the comparability of Ideas among themselves, in other words, with logic. We get a world in which the sole realities are Ideas or Universals existing independently of the thinker according to logical laws—the idealism of Hegel. But such a world exists independently of the subject. We are therefore back at a completely objective world, having started out in pursuit of a completely subjective one. And we are all ready to start out on another circle.

Like Fabre's processionary caterpillars on the rim of a jam jar, we can walk that circle again and again, the most dreary captivity of thought. It is one that every philosopher has hitherto been doomed to tread, and now bourgeois physics is treading it too. It is the circle of thought divorced from action: the cage of *pure* reason.

(*c*) No attempts to heal the dualism by combining the two positions have been successful. Any such compromises forcibly fly apart. The simplest compromise, that of Hume, Kant, Mach, Avenarius and the neo-realists, is to assert that phenomena (or sensa) are primary, that is, exist by themselves. But it is impossible to carry through such an argument logically, for the phenomena become completely lawless, they are simply a heap of relations, which we can take any way. Imagine a fabric being spun by a loom. If we snip the threads close to the shuttles, the whole weaving process becomes confusion, there is no pattern. How can colour generate size, size beauty, or beauty logic without the basis of the material object or subject? Such a world is not a subject either of discussion or thought, it is a mere chance collocation. The laws of science or thought are then simply convenient methods of enumerating these phenomena. One method is as good as another. There is no question of differing degrees of truth or reality. There is no meaning in the query whether one statement is *truer* than another. The most that can be claimed is that one is more economical—but it may be economical of paper, breath, thought, or bodily energy, and therefore in a paper shortage science might be completely transformed in all its hypotheses. This is not irony; it is a true statement of the Machian-Kantian position. A diagram may illustrate the problem.

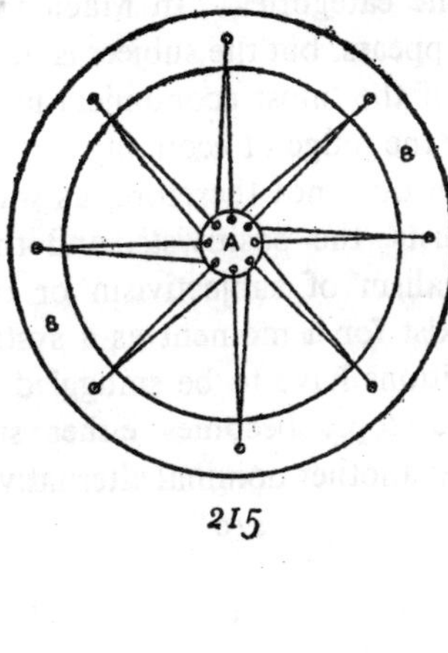

The centre disc, A, is the subject. The outer disc B, is the object. The threads represent the relations between them, or the phenomena. The whole system is the developing Universe. The pattern is all formed by one thread which, running through every hole, weaves the continuous intricate system. By declaring that only phenomena are real, phenomenalism, in all its forms, snips off these threads at the holes, and it is now no longer possible to understand the laws of their spacing, tension, or interweaving.

Not all relations are known, and conscious, but by following the endless thread, we come on new relations. We follow its course by means of action to change the object whose results, summarised in scientific laws, express objective reality in terms of thought and are able to predict the course of the thread. Thus phenomenalism (positivism) is anti-scientific, for it gives us no reason to suppose that the Universe of phenomena need be linked by any relations. On the contrary such relations are declared to be unknowable. The linkage is provided by the material basis of phenomena, and positivism denies the knowability of this matter.

So clear is this difficulty, that positivism is never carried out thoroughly to the end. In Kant's critical idealism, the object is smuggled in as the unknowable thing-in-itself, and the subject as 'the categories'. In Mach the unknowable Ding-an-Sich reappears, but the subject is now smuggled in under the form of the 'most economical laws of thought', the subject being the judge of economy.

Phenomenalism does not therefore, as was supposed by the critical idealists, the positivists, and the neo-realists, reconcile the dualism of subjectivism or objectivism. It cannot in fact exist for a moment as a system, and either one or both positions have to be smuggled in, so that the system, as it develops, becomes either subjectivism or objectivism, or yet another nominal alternative. If a relation between two terms exists, *i.e.* if the reality is A plus B, it is possible to take either A, or B, or (and this is the position of phenomenalism), we may take the *plus* alone, and claim to be reconciling the dualism. But of course we are not. We are forced in practice to join one party or the other.

(*d*) The final alternative is to omit the plus altogether. How then explain the knowledge by B of A, and the effect shown by A of B's actions upon A. By something that is neither B nor A, something that is outside reality—*i.e.* God. This is the philosophy of Descartes and Leibnitz. Spinoza's system has certain affinities with it, and chiefly differs in its resolute monism. According to such philosophers A and B function entirely separately, and the congruity of these functioning—Man knowing the world by thought and the world showing traces of Man's action on it—is explained by the fact that they were arranged beforehand by God, like elaborate mechanisms, so to run in time. In such a world, if the system is consistently carried out, no qualities are real, for neither subjective (mental) qualities, nor objective (material) qualities are primary. All are generated by God. The only real qualities therefore are the absolute qualities of theology—Omniscience, Omnipotence, Perfect Love, and so forth. Man and the world of colour, hope, and life are simply a shadow-show. But just as the stripping of the subjective element from objective qualities reduces them to mere equations, and the reverse process reduces them to logic, so the elimination of both subjective and objective elements in the qualities of a world from which the relations have already been excluded, leaves us with nothing but the fact that these elements are produced by an unknown outside term, or 'First Cause'. Even the theological attributes of God vanish, and we have only the uncaused Cause—another name for the self-determined primary term, which was given in our premises. We simply take out again the empty thing we put in.

Why does thought torment itself with this dualism, selecting every possible combination, yet thrown always back upon itself? And what is the solution? The second question will be answered first. The solution is dialectical materialism. Dialectical materialism goes behind subject and object to the material basis from which their antagonism arose.

(*e*) A and B, and the relations between them, are all real. The Universe is one, and is as a whole absolutely self-determined, but no part of it is absolutely self-determined. All that is real exists, and all that is real is determined, that is, every part of the Universe is in mutually determining A-B relations with the rest of the Universe. Everything therefore is knowable, for the meaning of knowable is simply this, the possibility of expressing a determining relation between that unknown but knowable thing, and a thing already known. This possibility is given in our premises.

This is our premise: that the Universe is a material unity, and that this is a becoming.

This material unity of becoming cannot be established by thought alone. It is established by thought in unity with practice, by thought emerging from practice and going out into practice. Phenomena are exhibited by the thing-in-itself, and if we can by practice force the thing-in-itself to exhibit phenomena according to our desire, then we know this much about the thing-in-itself—that in certain circumstances it will exhibit certain phenomena.

This is positive knowledge about the thing-in-itself. When we can in practice achieve all possible transformations we have all possible knowledge about the thing-in-itself. Thus we prove that the universe is a material unity by proving in practice the material basis of all phenomena.

This material basis is the thing-in-itself, or the like content of any phenomena exhibited by the thing-in-itself. This proof of material unity is secured by change and is therefore a process of becoming, of differentiation, of the emergence of the new. But it is a proof of unity, of the sameness, likeness, or determinism in all phenomena.

'The point is to change the world, not to interpret it.' For it is not possible to interpret the world, except by changing it. Thus the impasse of philosophers is seen to be the impasse of philosophy, and a proof of the impossibility of interpreting the world by thought alone.

A-B do not exist as eternally discrete entities. The Universe is a becoming, a development. The becoming is primary. Reality does not become *in* time and space, but time and space are aspects of its becoming. Becoming is change. If a thing is changed, it manifests an unlike, a hitherto non-present quality. If change is real, and by our premises it is primary, such a quality does not come into existence either by the gradual decrement of a known quality to nothing, or the gradual increment of a very faint quality to something. Before, it was not, not in any way. Now it is, in every way. There has therefore been a 'jump'. To deny this is to deny the reality of change, and to suggest that the quality was already there, but so faintly we did not 'notice it'. But nothing new would then have come into being. There would therefore have been no change, and reality is, by our definition, change.

Although such a quality is new, it is not arbitrary, *i.e.* absolutely self-determined. By definition the Universe is one. A quality that is self-determined is, as we saw, unknowable. Therefore each new quality, as it leaps into existence, is determined by all qualities up till then present in the universe.

These qualities do not come into being in time. Time does

not flow on while they emerge. The emergence of such qualities is what time is. Time then is an aspect of, or abstraction from, change. Time is new quality as it emerges.

But change does not merely involve the coming into existence of qualities. If we find different qualities lying about, even though they mutually determine each other, we cannot say 'something has changed'. The qualities may be qualities of different things, and so there will have been no change. There must therefore be something in all qualities that remains the same, even though these qualities are new, otherwise we cannot say, the 'Universe has changed'. There must be something like in all unlikes. Otherwise we could say, 'these unlikes are not *changed* things, they are *different* things. We have not moved in time, but in space.' How else can we distinguish motion in time from motion in space, unless time is not something in which things change, but the change itself?

But if the newness of quality, the unlikeness, as it emerges, is time, the oldness, the likeness, is space. Qualities do not arrange themselves homogeneously in space, space is the homogeneity in their qualities. Space is quantity or known quality as it remains unchanged; it is therefore the thing-in-itself, the material unity of the Universe. The Universe is a spatial Universe. Space therefore is an aspect of matter, which is precisely what relativity physics has established by practice. Mass-energy, or the likeness in phenomena, generates space. This is established by practice.

All laws of development, of evolution, of difference, of quality, of æsthetics, of consciousness, are temporal. All laws of conservation, of metrics, of comparability, of universal and unchanging relations, are spatial.

But time and space are only aspects of becoming or change. If we could completely abstract time or space, and divide relations into a set entirely temporal, and a set entirely spatial, we should have two absolutely self-determined spheres, contradicting our premises for each sphere would be unknowable to the other sphere. Therefore no absolute time or space, as premised in Newtonian dynamics, exists. We know both time and space and prove this by their mutual convertibility, by the change of qualities and the reproduction of quantities.

Neither does an absolute spatio-temporal *continuum* expressible in purely metrical terms exist. Such a continuum would after all be purely spatial, for it would be expressible entirely in terms of quantity. It would be self-determined, and independent of all quality. It would therefore be unknowable to quality, and quality would be unknowable to it. Hence Einstein's relativity physics still contains an illegitimate absolute, which accounts for its being irreconcilable with quantum phenomena.

We take as our premise 'becoming', the becoming of a material unity which is generated by our transformation of matter. Becoming, which involves change, which involves like and unlike, involves also *development*. If we had no develolpment, we would have no 'becoming'. In development there is a relation between the qualities A, B, C, D, E, which is not only mutually determining, but such that A is in some way contained in B, B in C, C in D, and D in E, but not E in D, D in C, C in B, B in A. This relation, which is technically called 'transitive but assymetrical', is involved in the process of becoming, just as are the existence of like and unlike. If becoming were otherwise, if qualities could not all be ranged in this unique order, we should come upon groups of qualities such, for example, that A would be contained in B, and then B in A; or in some other way there would be a 'break', or return to a quality in which all the new qualities of the interim no longer appear. But such a return is indistinguishable from the previous situation, and therefore we no longer have a process of becoming, but of unbecoming. Moreover the relation of containing and being-contained is, in development, mutually determining. If therefore the series of qualities (or events) in any way returns on itself in this fashion, the Universe splits in two 'in time'. We have two or more sets of self-determined qualities, sufficient to themselves, each unknowable and non-existent to the other.

We now see that the determination of qualities as they appear is a relation of a special sort. It is a transitive assymetrical relation known as 'cause and effect', in which one quality mutually determines another in a way which may be described as the containing (or sublation) of one quality in another. And all qualities (or events) may, by this means, be ranged in a unique order.

Moreover since no set of qualities is self-determined, we can never have a set of distinguishable qualities such that A *alone* determines or is contained in B; B *alone* determines or is contained in C, and so on, otherwise the series A, B, C, would be self-determined and unknowable. This would only be permissible if this series were the Universe. But we do not regard the Universe as composed of one event at a time. We do not believe that, whatever cross-section we took of the mass of qualities that we call the Universe, we would reveal over all the sections one quality only. If we could do that, space would then be separable from time, and we could collect spatial and temporal qualities in self-determined sets, which is contrary to our premises and experience. This cross-section would correspond to a universal or absolute present, which is permitted to Newtonian dynamics but is rightly eliminated from relativity physics.

Since then this series is impermissible, the qualities are always arranged as follows: A and A^1 contained in B. B and

B_1, contained in C. A^2 and A^3 contained in B_1. The only arrangement which will now completely satisfy all our premises is that each new quality, as it emerges, is determined by another quality (subject or *antithesis*) and the rest of the Universe (object or *thesis*). This does not apply merely to the qualities of cognition but to all events. In older formulations of causality, it would be stated that each 'event' (new quality) has a 'cause' (prior quality) and a 'ground' (the rest of the Universe). The ground is currently omitted for reasons of economy. For example, we say a bell is the cause of a sound. The air, earth, fixed stars must, however, be as they are in order for the bell to produce the sound. Any general scientific law must contain Universal constants. This is recognised by modern relativity physics (p) and quantum physics (h).

This then leads to the dialectical law of becoming, applicable to all qualities, that is, to all events. Any new quality, as it emerges, is determined by (or 'contains') a prior quality (the cause) and the rest of the Universe of qualities. Or, more strictly—since becoming its logically prior to time and space—the two terms determining a quality, (*a*) the prior quality and (*b*) all other determining qualities, are to that quality cause and ground, and contain its past time and its surrounding space. All other qualities not contained in this way, are part of its effect, and contain its future time. It is this relation which enables us to settle causality and time and space, which are never absolute, but relative to a quality.

Logically we express this as follows. Every new quality (B) is the synthesis of an opposition between (A) the cause, prior quality or *thesis*, and its negation (not-A), or *antithesis*—the rest of the Universe of qualities existent in relation to A. This dialectical movement does not take place in Time and Space, but Time and Space are abstractions from it.

Thus time not only is an abstraction of the unlikeness in in qualities, but is also and therefore the abstraction of the assymetrical relations between them which leave time open and 'infinite', and make its process and its arrangement unique, so that we cannot conceive the past in the future, or yesterday to-morrow, or ourselves going backwards in time. To go backwards in time would be to shed those qualities which contain the past, layer after layer, till we reach the past. But all that retraced 'shed' past, now no longer being in determining relations with the past-become-present, would cease to exist, and we should not have gone backwards in time. Or to go backwards in time would be to come again on to the qualities of the past which, contained in the present, now also contain the present, so that we revolve in a self-determined circle like a needle stuck in a gramophone record, and can therefore know nothing outside that circle, either past or future. We and the 'outside' would be non-existent to each other.

Space is not only an abstraction of the likeness in qualities, but it is also and therefore an abstraction of the symmetrical relations between them which make space closed and finite, and makes its process and its arrangement *non*-unique, so that we cannot conceive one part of space being *different* from another part, nor our being *unable* to retrace our steps over any distance we have traversed, just as we cannot conceive one part of time being *like* another part, nor of our being *able* to go back over any portion of time we have traversed. For if the qualities A, B, C, D, and E are assymetrically transitive, so that A is contained in B, B in C, and C in D, and D in A, there is a common relation to all events—in this particular series it is A, for if A is in B, and B is in C, and C is in D, and D is in E; A must be in E. A therefore is the spatial relation or likeness in development. It is that which develops, just as the unlike elements are the qualities exhibited by it in its development.

Every quality is an event; every event is a quality. Every quality of event is a relation between the subject A, and the object not-A—the rest of the Universe. The simplest quality (or event) is a quantum, in which there is a relation between the electron A, and the rest of the Universe not-A. Relations peculiar to A and general to the Universe must therefore both figure in the complete specification of a quantum. A quantum is the most temporal quality we can abstract, just as the interval is the most spatial.

Development does not take place *in* time and space. Development, becoming, and change, *secrete* time and space. Time and space are abstractions of it. Memory exhibits the assymetrical transitive relations we have mentioned, so does experience. They are therefore more concrete, nearer to reality and to becoming, than abstract time or space, or even the abstract spatio-temporal continuum. Learning, growth and evolution are not qualities absolutely peculiar to life; they are what we call becoming in its living aspects. Becoming includes both spatial finity and temporal infinity.

We now see that there is a universal dialectic of reality, a mode of movement which is prior to time, space, life and all other events and qualities. This dialectic proceeds as follows. First we have a quality. But a quality is a relation between subject and object, between A, subject, and not-A, the rest of the Universe. But the rest of the Universe not-A, has as its object A, to A it is subject and to it A is the rest of the Universe. The most 'primitive' quality we take therefore has two terms and a relation, this relation is involved in 'becoming' and ensures that the process of reality is open and 'infinite' at both ends.

Our most infinite regress into the past brings us therefore

to a quality, to an event. We cannot imagine anything simpler, for such a simplex one-term thing would be absolutely self-determined and could not be known-by-us, since knowing is a mutually determining relation between us and the thing. Any known event is already a quality, is already a subject-object relation. It already involves within itself an antagonism which can generate the means by which it is known.

We may take either term as primary and the other as dependent on it. Since we can take either term as primary, neither can be primary. They may be regarded as simultaneous. But they are not independent terms, for they are connected by a relation. The simplest quality therefore reveals itself as a subject-object relation. But the process of becoming involves that a new quality emerges (or event occurs) not by the increment of something already there, but abruptly, exhibiting something altogether unlike. But it also involves that this new state contains the first old quality in addition to the unlike new. This new state or quality is also analyseable as a two-term relation, and must in turn be succeeded by a new quality.

In other words, the fundamental mode of motion is a state, revealed to contain a thesis and an antithesis each of which is all that is not the other (are opposites), and yet neither are self-determined but are on the contrary, in mutually determining relation (unity of opposites). This is the thesis and antithesis. This state must give place to another, containing both the old quality (A and B) and yet an unlike element C. This is the synthesis. This quality, when it reveals its dualism, no longer reveals the dualism A and B, for this dualism parted between it (relation of subject to rest of Universe) the *whole* of reality. There is now newness, so therefore the same portioning of reality can no longer reveal the same dualism. The old dualism is therefore 'reconciled' in the new synthesis C, which itself however can now be analysed as a two-term relation, the foundation of another movement.

Quantity is the comparison of qualities among themselves. For this to be possible, they must all have a common element of likeness. Yet this likeness, constantly, by the dialectic movement, gives birth to the new. Quantity becomes quality, yet remains quantity. This movement guarantees the determinism of becoming, but not its predeterminism. The predeterminism of becoming is a nightmare arising from mechanical materialism.

This movement is not imposed on becoming by thought. It is the only way becoming can really become, conformably to our reason and experience; and it is in our reason because our experience is part of this becoming. This movement contains within it time and space, memory and perception, quality and quantity, all of which entities are abstractions from it. Time is the difference between synthesis and the preceding relation, space is the similarity between them. The dialectic movement of the Universe does not occur in space and time, it gives rise to them. The external world does not impose dialectic on thought, nor does thought impose it on the external world. The relation between subject and object, ego and Universe is itself dialectic. Man, when he attempts to think metaphysically, merely contradicts himself, and meanwhile continues to live and experience reality, *dialectically*.

Knowledge of reality can only be generated when subject and object attack each other dialectically, each changing the other in the process. The change of the object is man's transformation of nature. The change of the subject is knowledge. Thus dialectical materialism heals the subject-object dualism, not by denying one (idealism or mechanical materialism) or both (positivism) but by making this antagonism the creative source of knowledge, as an active relation in which both man's theory and practice are generated.

We thus see that the dualism that torments philosophy, the dualism between the mind and nature, between the subject and object, between the ego and the external world, is the analysis of a quality, or the two-term relation, which is not unique to mind but part of the process of becoming. The same dual relation describes the relation between a quantum and its surroundings. We make the problem needlessly difficult by making our 'A' term, not any particular human brain but men's brains in general, and 'not-A' not Nature at any particular time but nature throughout the past. The dialectic relation still retains its essential form, but is difficult to analyse fruitfully. It is quite legitimate to do this, but it is simpler to take one human brain in particular, or even a particular set of relations such as perception. The basic dialectic remains the same, and the analysis is now simpler.

The question of which is first, mind or matter, is not therefore a question of which is first, subject or object. Every discernment of a quality (mind, truth, colour, size) is the discernment of a two-term relation between a thing as subject and the rest of the Universe. Mind is the general name for a relation between the human body, as subject, and the rest of the Universe. The human body is a general name for a relation between the rest of the Universe, as subject, and the mind, as object. Mind is a loose name for such relations holding with all such human bodies (or including perhaps the bodies of animals) just as body is a loose name for such relations holding with all minds. Going back in the Universe along the dialectic of qualities we reach by inference a state where no human or animal bodies existed and therefore no minds. It is not strictly accurate to say that therefore the object is prior to the subject any more than it is correct to say the opposite. Object and subject, as exhibited by the mind relation, come into being simultaneously. Human body, mind, and human environment cannot exist separately, they are all parts of the one set. What is prior is the material unity from which they arise as an inner antagonism.

We can say that relations seen by us between qualities in our environment (the arrangement of the cosmos, energy, mass, all the entities of physics) existed before the subject-object relationship implied in mind. We prove this by the transformations which take place independent of our desires. In this sense nature is prior to mind and this is the vital sense for science. These qualities produced, as cause and ground produce effect, the synthesis, or particular subject-object relationship which we call knowing. Nature therefore produced mind. But the nature which produced mind was not nature 'as seen by us', for this is importing into it the late subject-object relationship called 'mind'. It is nature as known by us, that is, as having indirect not direct relations with us. It is nature in determining relation with, but not part of, our contemporary universe. Yet, by sublation, this nature that produced mind is contained in the universe of which the mind relation is now a feature; and that is why it is known to us.

Such a view of reality reconciles the endless dualism of mentalism or objectivism. It is the Universe of dialectical materialism. Unlike previous philosophies it includes all reality; it includes not only the world of physics, but it includes smells, tastes, colours, the touch of a loved hand, hopes, desires, beauties, death and life, truth and error. In such a view all things pass away, for all things must change, and yet nothing passes away, for the past is sublated in the future. Such a world is finite and infinite; it contains both.

All other philosophies split on this rock, that they contain self-determined spheres of qualities, whether this be the continuum of Einstein (for relativity physics is a philosophy) or the world of Ideas of Plato, or the world of sensory data of Berkeley, or the world of 'values' of axiologists. But one is then driven into the difficulty that here on the one side one has a self-determined sphere of values, tensors, ideas, or sensa, not in relation with all other nameable qualities on the other side. Therefore one of these two spheres is primary and real, and the other secondary and unreal, or not *really* real. In the world of physics for instance, smells, colours, hardnesses and shapes are not *really* real. But the reality of dialectical materialism is competent to include all these qualities as real, for all are in mutually determining relations with each other. There is no closed world of art, physics, morals, or mind. All these worlds are open, and are part of the one causality and process; and of no quality must it be said 'this is an appearance or an illusion'. Such a world includes as real not only all truths, but all errors, yet error remains opposed to and distinguishable from truth. Such a world includes future and past, but the future remains opposed to and distinguishable from the past.

Moreover, such a world of reality, although it contains all qualities and all experience and has no closed parts, is yet *as a whole* self-determined. It requires for its movement no unknowable forces, general indeterminism, or mysterious gods. It is free in itself. Precisely because it contains in itself no closed worlds and in it truth and error, being and not-being, mutually determine each other, it is not itself determined. Such a Universe is therefore monistic and pluralistic, just as it is finite and infinite. Its future is not fully predictable, because if the unlikenesses in qualities were predictable, they would not be new. But its future is fully determined, because if the quantities of the future were not like those of the present it would no longer be one Universe of becoming.

In such a Universe thought is real; it plays a real rôle; but matter is real. Thought is a relation of matter; but the relation is real; it is not only real but determining. It is real *because* it is determining. Mind is a determining set of relations between the matter in my body and in the rest of the Universe. It is not all the set, for not all the necessities whereby my body and the rest of the Universe mutually determine each other is known to me, not all my being is conscious being. In so far as these relations are conscious, I am free, for to be free is to have one's conscious volition, determine the relations between the Universe and oneself. The more these relations between my body and the Universe are part of my conscious volition the more I am free. These relations are necessary or determining relations. Freedom is the consciousness of necessity.

This is the theory of dialectical materialism which is itself the outcome of a dialectical movement. A philosophy is generated in society and is therefore the outcome of a social movement. The early mechanical materialism of Descartes and Hobbes, strengthened by Condillac and d'Holbach and accepted as the official methodology of physics, produced its opposite, idealism, and this reached its climax with absolute idealism. Absolute idealism is the apex of bourgeois philosophy, and all succeeding philosophies are either pedestrian recapitulations of earlier philosohpies or simple eclecticism. There has been no noteworthy bourgeois philosopher since Hegel. For these two opposing bourgeois philosophies, by their very contradictions, gave rise to their synthesis, dialectical materialism. This was the outcome of classical bourgeois philosophy. It synthesised these elements not by a rigid formalism but by proceeding *beyond* philosophy, by becoming a sociology and exhibiting how both mechanical materialism and objective idealism were generated, as a social product, in social action upon reality through economic production.

Dialectical materialism was itself an outcome of the contradictions of capitalist economy. When communism and dialectical materialism emerged, all the discoveries of bourgeois science that made such a view of the Universe necessary now began to distort the framework of bourgeois culture, so that it could no longer hold the forces it had generated and bourgeois theory became a brake instead of an aid to action and discovery. Relativity and quantum physics, experimental psychology, evolution and genetics, anthropology, comparative religion, are a few of the disruptive forces in modern culture, which necessarily give rise to semi-dialectical philosophies, to incomplete attempts at synthesising the anarchy of bourgeois thought. The characteristic of the relation of bourgeois theory to practice in science is, that the more general the theory, the more it is a hindrance to practice; the more detailed and particular it is, the less it acts as a distorting force.

* * * * *

Neo-Realism (or neo-Platonism) is, in its various forms, but a late development of phenomenalism or positivism. Concepts of 'organisation', entelechy, closed spheres of value and the like, merely represent the veering of positivism towards objective idealism and mentalism. It is easy enough to see that such philosophies do not heal dualism, and do not give any thorough-going reality to all classes of experience. Whitehead, Russell, the gestalt psychologists, Eddington, Jeans, Broad, and the many others only differ in their capacities for logic, or the narrowness of their aims and content. It is not really possible to sit on the fence in bourgeois dualism. Sooner or later one finds oneself on one side and to-day that side is always idealism, never mechanical materialism. Of course such late bourgeois idealism has never the scope or coherence of Hegelian Idealism, just because all the old confidence has gone. The bourgeois no longer really believes in himself or his theory.

Morgan and Alexander may be bracketed as leaders of a popular philosophy which really found its pioneer in Spencer and its most subtle exponent in Bergson. Impressed by the fact of biological evolution, a concrete proof of the transformability of matter, that life has a dialectical history, such philosophers attempt to forge a dialectical 'theory of life' which takes the following form: New unpredictable qualities appear as jumps. Thus, 'liquidity' represents one jump, 'life' another, 'mind' a third, and so forth. These qualities *emerge*.

Such a philosophy collapses, however, because these qualities, or jumps, are *imposed*. They do not result from qualities which are two-termed relations, whose terms, by their repulsion, created the synthetic quality that 'emerges'. Mind is a simple one-term quality without relation; such qualities are not therefore after all *real*. In spite of the desperate attempts of such philosophers to save sensory data, sensa remain secondary and unreal. Moreover time and space are not the dialectical change. They are (according to Alexander) the matrices in which the change takes place. As with Plato, space is the womb of all becoming.

Thus, instead of a world of becoming in which all unfolds itself with complete determinism, because all phenomena are materially real, we have a world unfolded in time and space by the Jack-in-the-box appearance of new and unpredictable qualities. Such a philosophy is incompetent to explain society or the generation either of itself or other philosophies. It cannot heal dualism.

It gives rise to the question, if these qualities are not determined but imposed, who imposes them? We thus return to a very early philosophy, to a god determining but Himself self-determined, outside the Universe, who arbitrarily pumps in these qualities into a passive world. It makes no difference whether, as with Bergson, such a god exists now or, as with Alexander, such a god exists in the future and is continually attracting these qualities out of the world, as the sun raises blisters on the skin.

These new bourgeois evolutionary philosophies which start out to be dialectical and scientific, end by being less so than the older bourgeois philosophies. The world becomes an amorphous mass lying in Time and Space with no determining relations between its phenomena, for all values are imposed upon it in an arbitrary way, as if it were a piece of dough. Such philosophies fail in their primary motive, that of synthesising bourgeois philosophy. Should anyone wish to have the melancholy proof of this, they need only read Alexander's *Space, Time and Deity*, which proves his philosophy to be inadequate even to contain relativity physics.

Indeed, unless such a philosophy can penetrate to the seat of bourgeois dualism—its genesis in the society that produced it—it cannot escape from dualism. it cannot reconcile dualism, any more than the separate boughs of a tree can be 'reconciled' if we cannot see the trunk. Mechanical materialism and absolute idealism represent the extremest possible antitheses of bourgeois dualism, and any philosophy which does not reconcile them is doomed to be a less *logical* philosophy. Bergson is as good an example as any of the bourgeois who, striving to escape from bourgeois categories, in fact falls back into them. He attempts to describe an evolutionary world, but at the end, all he has is a static world, whose mass is moved on by an external *élan vital.* He attempts to describe a world in which Time is real, because the past is conserved in the present. But his past conserved in the present is a world in which Time is unreal, because the qualities which make the past present are not temporal, they are products of an outside force, *Life*, and Time therefore becomes merely the empty stage of their exhibition.

Bergson attempts to describe a world in which mind has significance, and is real, but he creates a world in which mind, because it is separate from matter and plays on it as organ, is a *complete* machine *without* mind. All sensa, all values, and all qualities are *either* not in the world, and are therefore an unreal façade, *or* are in the world, in which case they are not mental. He endeavours to pose intuition as a synthesis of instinct and intelligence. He attempts to escape from metaphysical dualism, and the weakness of formal logic—that nothing emerges which is not already there—but he only does so by demarcating instinct and intelligence as if they were entirely separate things. But this is not so; all instincts have intelligent modifications, and are conditioned by experience. All intelligence utilizes organic instruments (the brain, existing reflexes). The difference is a matter of degree. By making it *absolute*, Bergson achieves as his new term, *intuition.* What is his intuition? Exactly what he is trying to escape from—scholasticism! Intuition, as Bergson visualises it, solves problems 'by pure thought', and not as problems are in fact solved—by instinct, modified by experience, becoming increasingly conscious and therefore increasingly *intelligent.* Now this solving of problems without modification by practice, is precisely the method of metaphysics and logic—of all the rationalism which Bergson rightly condemns for its sterility. Thus Bergson's intuition is not a synthesis of two contradictions. The contradiction is not between instinct and intelligence, but between instinctive action and conscious thought, and the synthesis is science, a positive activity which on the one hand changes, the world to man's instinctive desires and, on the other hand changes man by making him more conscious of reality. But Bergson, revolting against metaphysics, produces simply an extreme form of rationalism, his 'intuition'.

All these late bourgeois philosophies fail in this one elementary requirement:

(1) 'Do they explain (that is, *include*) all the scientific discoveries of their era, in the one framework?'

Not one of them is competent to do this. There are two other requirements:

(2) 'Do they include, as real and unified, all forms of experience—colours, sounds, values, aims, time, space and change?'

(3) 'Do they account, not only for these, but for the evolution of all the various arts, sciences, and religions in their historical evolution, and for their own explanation of them? In other words, do they explain not only the objects of experience, but the evolution of explanations of these objects, both in their truth and their falsity?'

Obviously a philosophy which achieves these goals has transformed itself into a sociology, but it is a measure of the poverty of bourgeois philosophy that not only does it fail in all attempts at solving the first question, but the very need to solve the other two hardly presents itself. When one views, in their contemporary cultures, the achievements of Descartes, Locke, Spinoza, Kant and Hegel, it is possible to realise how far-reaching has been the dissolution of bourgeois culture. It is even possible for M. Maritain, speaking as a Thomist, to hurl insults at contemporary bourgeois philosophy:

'The drama of Western culture consists in the fact that its

stock of common metaphysics has been reduced to an utterly inadequate minimum, so that only matter holds it together, and matter is incapable of keeping anything together.'

It is not either matter or metaphysics that is responsible for the decomposition of bourgeois culture, but the social anarchy rooted in its economy. But whatever the cause, this decomposition has now advanced to a stage where a Scholastic philosopher can reproach the bourgeois philosophers with a 'betrayal' of reason and with an 'incoherent' world-view. Would not Newton, Galileo, Bacon and Descartes turn in their graves if they knew the time had come when a medievalist could reproach their heirs with a 'betrayal of reason'? Nothing could reveal more clearly the retrogression of bourgeois philosophy.

Because bourgeois intellectual confusion is rooted in the form of society of which it is a product, it cannot attain to the consistent world-view of dialectical materialism without seeing what is the law of motion of this society that produces bourgeois philosophy, and what will be its outcome. But when one has seen that, one has ceased to be bourgeois; one no longer stands in one's own light and can see bourgeois culture clearly. One has become a Communist.

* * * * *

This transition, which involves understanding in oneself all the formulas and conventions imposed by one's bourgeois upbringing and deriving therefrom something more fundamental, is not easy. Thus many even of those people who see clearly the bankruptcy of capitalism, and the analytical power of Marxism, are unable to grasp the synthesis. They remain bourgeois, and therefore they impose on themselves the task of 'improving' or 'modifying' dialectical materialism. They propose to bring it 'up-to-date', by modifying it according to the lessons learned from recent scientific development.

They do not see that such a programme is simply one of making dialectical materialism bourgeois—making it moreover not *classical* bourgeois, which could merely mean dissolving it into the Hegelianism or mechanical materialism of which it is the outcome, but *degenerate* bourgeois, making it Bergsonian or Machian. They do not see that the task *vis-à-vis* dialectical materialism and the latest developments of bourgeois science is not that of bringing dialectical materialism up to date, but that of bringing these anarchic developments up to date by synthesising them in the consistent world-view of Marxism. This is obvious, for on the one hand one has a coherent system—dialectical materialism —and on the other hand one has a chaotic confusion of 'discoveries'—relativity physics, quantum physics, Freudism, anthropology, genetics, psycho-physiology, which are based on exclusive assumptions and contradict or ignore each other. If there is to be any relation between these two groups at all, obviously dialectical materialism must impose its coherence on the mish-mash, and not the mish-mash its incoherence on dialectical materialism. The second programme is simply pointless. It would be better to leave things as they are.

Of course in practice all who set themselves the second programme perform it in a typically bourgeois way. Whatever the particular closed world of bourgeois ideology they inhabit—physics, psychology, economic, philosophy, art, or religion—it is the limited and exclusive categories of that world they would enforce on the universal categories of dialectical materialism. The dialectical materialism so 'improved' is not only therefore now inadequate to take in all the other closed worlds that this particular bourgeois renovator does not inhabit, but soon proves itself as incapable as ordinary bourgeois philosophy of dealing completely even with the closed world in which resides the expert in modernising. Necessarily so, for the closed world is just the characteristic of bourgeois bankruptcy.

To return to the question with which this essay began: Can physics, in its final stages of relativity, be restored to the world of real experience? Can I, as I live, remember, think, move, see and act, find in that concrete immediate experience the refined concepts of relativity physics? Not only can I, but I *must*, for relativity physics is extracted from perception and experience, just as is Newtonian physics. The fall of an apple, the passage of light, the motion of earth and sun, the weight of objects, all these experienced *perceived* realities gave a common content to Newtonian and Einsteinian hypothesis. But there was also a difference, and this too owed its existence to an experience—to the Michelson-Morley experiment. And the confirmation of the later theory was due to experience, to seen things, the precession of the perihelion of Mercury, the bending of light rays by gravitation, and the gain in mass of w particles. Therefore all the entities of this physics whose form could be determined by experience, must exist in experience.

I live, therefore I think I am. I have experience whether I perceive or reflect and this is common to both feelings, that *I endure*. 'I,' a thing that remains unchanged. But this 'I' endures; it *lives*. It sees, suffers, thinks of things that are not the same, for sometimes it has suffering, sometimes joy. Sometimes it sees one thing, sometimes another. And yet it is always the 'I', the unchanging thing, that sees and suffers. So that this always like 'I', is also unlike; continually, new things emerge and yet my perception of these things shows the same element in their behaviour to me. They too endure, and yet they change. Always there is a like perpetually manifesting unlike; continually there is unlikeness revealing a like. This is experience, or *becoming*.

Becoming, because I *remember*. First I suffered, then I rejoiced, then I feared. Suffering, I did not know of the rejoicing or the fear. Rejoicing, I 'remembered' the suffering, it tinged my rejoicing; but I did not yet know fear. Fearing at last, I remembered that I had rejoiced with a memory of suffering, and suffered but with no memory of fear or rejoicing. All my feelings could be arranged in that order, in which the subsequent included memories of the precedent, but not *vice versa*. This order of feelings I called 'Time'. Every item in it had this unlikeness which yet could by memory range them in a unique order.

But not my perceptions of things. These things had an order among themselves. I could go to a thing, and then walk to another thing, and then it appeared that, exactly retracing my steps, I could come on the original thing. *Exactly retracing my steps*; here was a difference. For I could experience a thing; then experience another thing; then return to the original thing and yet remember not only my experience of another thing, but my earlier experience of the original thing. Thus I had no unique endless order, but a closed order which I could repeat in endless ways. All these repetitions, these recurrences, could be ranged in this likeness upon unlikeness. I called this 'Space'.

And now I was able to distinguish more sharply between my own feelings, which were always in Time, in a unique order, and things, which were ranged in Space, in an order not unique but closed.

I was inclined to separate Time from Space, and my feelings from things; but this was wrong. They were different; they were opposite; but how could I say they were exclusive, for the relations between them were just what experience was? Every experience contained a *feeling*, a newness, a knowledge that Time had moved on, and a *thing*, an oldness, a knowledge that I had met this before. I who had the feelings of difference, yet remained I. I remained I because I myself was a thing—a body. The *things*, whose relations remained repeatable and non-unique, *caused* the change in my *feelings*. Every experience contained subject and object, time and space. I discovered I could never separate them in experience. How could the statement that they were absolutely separate therefore have meaning? Moreover Time and space always contained an experience or relation between things. How then could the statement that things had relations *in* Time and Space, conceived as neutral containers, have meaning? It was just my experience in my relations with things, which gave me my ideas of time-relations and space-relations. How could these relations exist without terms, as things-in-themselves? If I made this mistake (and for a time I did make it) it was one for which I had no warrant. It led me into all kinds of paradoxes, so I gave it up, and set out to measure and classify and compare, not happenings *in* Time and Space, but the time and space *in* happenings.

How did I carry out this important task? First of all by the invention of numbers. All qualities, all elements in the flux of experience, are *becoming*. There is a likeness, a something that changes, and an unlikeness, the changefulness of this thing. Moreover there are not merely bundles of likeness and unlikeness, but all qualities can be arranged in a unique order, such that event A is 'memorably' contained in B, event B in C, event C in D. This 'nesting' of events involves that there is something common to all events. Thus, in the series just named, quality A is common to all events. Experience never finds an end to the events in either direction.

This gives us the series of integers; 1, 2, 3, 4, 5, etc. The series is dialectic; each number synthesises (memorably contains) every previous number, and yet contains a new quality, for how otherwise could we differentiate it? This series is thus adequate to describe all quantities, for it describes the essential process of becoming.

But the series is not unique. 2 may be determined by 1 and 1, or $\frac{1}{2}$ and $\frac{3}{2}$, and so on. Each quality is then the limit of an infinite number of different possible series.

Let us take two things—two *likenesses.* We take a thing *here*, where I am now, and a thing *there* where I am not now. We measure the number of like events between these things. For example we ourselves pace backwards and forwards (9 steps on each journey, 9 events). This is a like relation. The original thing returned to after our pacing has changed, but because there is a likeness recogniseable beneath the change we call it 'the same thing'.

Thus space becomes a relation between ourself and things. We pace between things. We never find distance except as a relation between ourselves and things (ourselves pacing, measuring, and watching). Distance becomes the measurement of like events among themselves by us.

Just because the two sets of nine like events also had an element of unlike and were arranged inclusively in our memory in the series 1-9 and 10-18, they were valid as a measurement of like things. Thus we find an element of unlikeness in all our relations of like things determining them. Time always figures in space.

We decide to find how *little* time need figure in space. Time is the element of unlikeness, what is the minimum? In the pacing of like events forward or back between things, there is always this unlikeness. The fewer the events, the less the unlikeness. We find that of all relations involving likeness and unlikeness, the light ray can mediate between things with the least unlikeness in contemporary events.

This relation, the light relation, is therefore the most spatial relation between events. It is a minimum relation. A minimum relation is unique. We therefore have a minimum relation which, when it occurs between two things, involves the least element of unlikeness between all other related qualities in the world. This minimum relation we call *zero interval*, but, discovering the same relation in a different sphere, we call this minimum relation the *quantum*. Zero interval is the least unlikeness in the universe which will differentiate 'between' things, and make them different in space. The quantum is the least unlikeness in things which will integrate a thing and make it the same in time.

What is the most temporal relation? It is that relation which has the most likeness in it. But we recognise things as 'knots' of likeness. Therefore the greatest possible likeness in relations inheres *within* what we call a thing. While qualities are emerging in experience, those which show most likeness have as their relation maximum interval, which is the most spatial relation. We say, *this thing follows a geodesic*. The geodesic relation is the relation a thing's qualities have among themselves and therefore it is the most temporal relation. Discovering the same relation in a different sphere, we call it an *electron*.

But now we close the circle. This likeness is only evidenced in a bunch of relations. It is an *intersection* of qualities; the most like element in them. But in each quality, because we can distinguish between the qualities, there is an unlikeness. The electron never exists in itself, always it is manifesting unlikenesses. But the light interval, although it connects two *different* things, yet *connects* them, and therefore is the result of an element of likeness in its opposed terms.

*   *   *   *   *

What world follows from all this?

(*a*) Time and space are the way we sort the qualities in which material things participate. Each sorting is different for each thing; therefore each has its own time and space. There is nothing outside this emergence of qualities, not even relations, for every quality contains a subject, a relation, and an object (the rest of the universe). These qualities are discontinuous and have a minimum, the quantum or the light ray, and a maximum, the characteristic of following a geodesic and being matter, but neither is separate from the other. The quantum is the unit of time, the electron of space, but each is involved in the other, each emerges from the one material becoming of experience.

All these qualities, according to their difference and likeness, can be sorted in a unique series: *i.e.* the Universe is *completely* determined. The series nowhere holds back on itself; no sphere is self-determined. The series is not time; time merges from the subject-object analysis; time is contained in the series, but only as the 'perspective' of one particle. This is true also of space.

Time, like space, is three-dimensional (past, present, future). But because time is an accretion of unlikenesses, these three dimensions always distinguish themselves. Those of space must be distinguished, because space is an accretion of likenesses. That is why wave mechanics requires six dimensions to describe the relation of two electrons, for there is never a relation between two electrons only, but between an electron and the rest of the world.

This is the world of experience as seen by dialectical materialism. It is not only a world of experience, but also a world of biology, psychology, sociology, art and physics. Not only is it the world of relativity physics, but it is also, and at the same time, the world of quantum physics.

The world, in the process of becoming, exhibits an accumulation of unlikeness. Likeness has as one aspect *organisation.* This increase of unlikeness appears therefore, as an increase of disorganisation. This is the 'entropy gradient', the basis of the Second Law of Thermodynamics.

It is maintained by bourgeois physics, however, that a Universal return from disorder to order, *i.e.* a return of the series from A includes B, B includes C, to C includes B is not impossible, but only grossly improbable. This is based on a misunderstanding, due to the concept of Time as the matrix of becoming.

Time is in fact the inclusive series of unlike qualities such that A includes B, and B includes C. Consequently it is by definition impossible to talk of such a series returning on itself in time, for Time is the non-returning of the series. The last of such a series that returned would be 'past'.

If anyone could define Time in any other way, so as to produce a more consistent world-view and upset our experience and the discoveries of relativity physics, then that would no longer be the case. But until they do reach such a formulation, no meaning can be assigned to a Universe which returns to a previous order from disorder. It is not extremely improbable, but impossible, for it is a contradiction in terms. If it happened, or could be shown to be possible, it would indicate, not only that our present definition of Time is wrong but also what Time really is.

The physicist, confronted by a small-scale infringement of the law—*e.g.* gas gathering into half of a receptacle and leaving the other in a vacuum, would reason in this way: 'Here is disorder becoming order, which is just what cannot happen since it means the time in this receptacle has, so to speak, gone backwards in comparison to my time. I therefore conclude that in fact it has not gone back, and that there is a subsequency about the local accumulation of a gas, which can only mean that it is *part* of a larger increase in unlikeness or disorder. In other words I must assume that this gas must have been acted upon by forces outside itself, and that there is an outside cause for this behaviour. If not, it is my time that has gone backwards, and I am living into the past. But this receptacle is too small for this to be a necessary deduction.'

The concept of entropy involves that the system in which entropy must increase is self-determined and therefore unknowable and non-existent. The second Law of Thermodynamics therefore only applies accurately to the whole Universe and the probability it measures is really the degree of its inaccuracy.

It follows from a dialectical world view that nothing is absolute and self-determined but the Universe itself. The complexity of men's conscious relations with the Universe may grow continuously, but they will never be co-incident with the Universe. Their very increase is the generation of new qualities which now form part of the unknown. Thus nothing is unknowable, because nothing is self-determined or unmediated, but absolute knowledge is unattainable. Every expression or vehicle of knowledge, every formulation of consciousness, is incomplete. It does not 'contain' an error, but its limited truth is determined by its limited error. The elimination of its error does not give us absolute truth: a new hypothesis is required synthesising them in an ampler statement. This can only come about if the error in the former hypothesis has been revealed in practice—if the contradiction implicit in it has become overt, and truth and error have flown asunder, generating a new truth. Man therefore learns by his mistakes. The discovery of an error is the discovery of a new truth, for, if the error is discoverable, the new truth is now knowable. This is the 'unity of truth and error', and it is not a 'mysticism' of dialectics, but is a description of a process common to the methodology of science and life.

Are we therefore, as dialectical materialists, supporters of Vaihinger's '*Als Ob*' * and the *value* of fictions? No, for to believe in the absolute value of error as an end is to be as limited as to believe in an absolute truth. In dialectics an error cannot be tolerated. The antagonism between truth and error is real. Once known, once this negation has revealed itself, the intolerableness of error prevents thought from resting upon it, and man moves on to a new truth. But according to Vaihinger, man is consciously content with error and rests on it. Thought loses its impetus. Vaihinger's view remains a metaphysical bourgeois doctrine. He is a positivist: his position is that reality is unknowable. Since entities are unknowable in themselves, everything that works is as true as it is possible for a thing to be true.

But dialectics, if it is to justify its programme, must explain the origin of this 'tired' bourgeois philosophy. It must leave no sphere self-determined. It must close the changing circle of being. Why has dualism wrecked bourgeois philosophy? Why was Platonism 'congealed' and not dialectical? Why is Marxism dialectical?

If no sphere is self-determined, ideology must be in a mutually determining relation with the society of which it is a product. They must fit each other, at every level, like hand and glove, like river and river bed, for philosophy is a social product. This arises from the very fact that we can talk about society. The private thoughts of an individual are inaccessible; the desires of a man to do something are invisible. But as soon as man's thoughts issue in language, in concepts, in a coherent system, they become social. They have adopted social forms: language and ideas, evolved by the process of society. Such a public system of thought is a social product. And as soon as man's desires to do something result in action, in the moulding of material into

* *The Philosophy of 'As If'*. (Kegan Paul.)

something socially recognised as having use and value, here too aim becomes end, desire becomes a social product. Thought and will are private and personal; a philosophy and a commodity are social products. Yet thought and will, though private, are determined by the philosophy and material products of the society into which a man is born. What I am taught and what I see round me, influence what I think about, and what I desire.

Thus thought is naturally dialectic in so far as it is part of the process of society. At each stage thought and material being are flung apart and return on each other, in mutual determinism, generating the new qualities of society. How then does thought become congealed? Bourgeois revolt gives rise to mechanical materialism. This in turn generates idealism. But these two opposites cannot be reconciled within the framework that produced them. All thought that remains within these two poles becomes non-dialectic. It becomes barren logic-chopping. The true synthesis is Marxism; but Marxism is revolutionary; it rests on a revolution of the class structure of society. *It is the class structure of society that is holding back the dialectical movement of thought.* The poverty of bourgeois philosophy is rooted in the breakdown of bourgeois economy. These outworn production relations are holding back the productive forces of society, holding back not merely the full produce of idle factory plants, derelict coffee plantations, unploughed fields and unemployed men, but of human brains.

* * * * *

We know the bourgeois illusion to be a reflex of the class structure of bourgeois society. The first stage is the bourgeois revolt: 'I am free in so far as I throw off all social restraint.' Man, by the insurgent exercise of his desires, can dominate his environment, not as master dominates slave—such relations are banned—not by a simple fiat of his will—but as an owner dominates his property, as a craftsman dominates his tool, a farmer his land—by knowing its laws. *The bourgeois sees the environment as his tool in the first stage of the bourgeois development.*

This first dialectic movement of the revolutionary bourgeoisie gives rise to Elizabethan tragedy, to the exploration of the world, to Spanish and Tudor moonarchy, to Galileo, to the splendid conation of the sixteenth and seventeenth centuries, finally to Newtonism and Cartesianism. The discovery of the 'law of gravity', of analytical geometry, of the farthest limits of the world, marks the crescendo of the bourgeois explosion into the environment. The bourgeois has now seized the environment as tool. The mechanical materialistic philosophy of Hobbes, Condillac, D'Holbach, and the like expresses the limit of the vast social movement which has already, in reaching the limit, clearly revealed its opposite. This is the apogee (1750) of the first stage of capitalism.

For from the environment, dominated as a tool in the extraverted, exploring period of social relations, we now pass to the bourgeois himself in the introverted analytical period. All the bourgeois acts of will at first flow into the environment, and are there realised. This is not in his opinion a determining relation, for the bourgeois is, by his initial revolution, free in himself. Because therefore this is not a mutually determining relation, because he knows as it were by simple inspection, he has no two-way connexion with his environment. *He has no guarantee that the environment known by him has an independent existence. If it determined his knowing, even as his knowing determined it, this would perforce constitute independent existence on its part.* But the bourgeois denies this! Hence Berkeley, Hume, Kant, Comte, and neo-positivism. In this second stage of bourgeois economy we have the birth of idealism. The environment either does not exist, or is unknowable. Mind is primary.

This development is the result of industrial capitalism, of the terrific power over its environment manifested by the machine. This makes it seem as if the mind is everything, and the environment nothing. It makes mind seem the sole active force generating all quality.

Society can only seem to be the success of individual will, in an economy in which men act as if their sole actions are undetermined and primary. The bourgeois producing for the market, free from all social control and restraint, believes that in doing what seems most to fulfil his will to profit, he is free. The market, the regulator of bourgeois economy, stands to him as environment, and shields him from reality.

In fact his actions are determined by the market and the market itself is determined by the completely blind actions of thousands of men like himself, but the law of its determinism is unknown to him. There is no control, no awareness of the relations between individual producers which determine slump and boom. Hence the bourgeois regards the success of society in changing the environment, not as the outcome of social laws, but as the outcome of free individual mind, as the success of personal conation. When he is sufficiently insulated from the environment by the development of his class, this becomes idealism.

Such an idealistic philosophy is necessarily the philosophy of a ruling class, with whom the environment seems to obey their free will as will. The proletariat cannot generate such a philosophy because this same capitalist economy exploits them. It forces them to bring their labour power into the market to sell to the best bidder or go empty away if there is none. Its anarchy makes them unfree. It does not fulfil their wills, it exploits them.

The proletariat has a remedy, that of social organisation. By combining into trade unions, and accepting social constraints, not haphazard but to a conscious end—higher wages, better conditions—the workers secure the fulfilment of their wills. And in the factories where they work, their organisation is what gives labour its productivity.

Thus the proletariat, generated by the exploitation of bourgeois economy, cannot accept any philosophy that sees freedom in lack of social organisation and constraint; the path of freedom, the road of fulfilment of desire. On the contrary, the only way they can realise their wills is by establishing, in bitter fight, the organisations and social restraints (Factory Acts, Right to Strike, etc.) which the bourgeois rejected. Thus the operation of bourgeois economy generates its negation in its exploited class.

But this negation is not a return to medieval philosophy, which bourgeois philosophy itself negated. Medieval social restraints were unconscious; their organisations were not planned to secure an end; they were rigid, inflexible, imposed from above. They did not represent mass co-operation but lord-and-slave domination. They were the product of a class society.

Thus the philosophy enforced on one by being a member of the proletariat, is higher than either feudal or bourgeois philosophy. It is nearer to reality; it includes them both. It includes the organisation embodied consciously in feudal society, but it does not permit these organisations to arise as expressions of the privilege of a ruling class. They arise from the needs of the co-operative task, just as to lift a huge rock necessitates co-operative action by a gang of men and this action is not imposed by a lord's will, but by the shape and weight of the stone and the nature of the tools available.

In Hegelianism the Idea becomes absolute, objective, and creates the whole world. This is the climax of bourgeois philosophy. Concurrently bourgeois economy is reaching its apex.

Up till then there had been no dualism in bourgeois philosophy, only the dialectic *yea* and *nay* of thought generating greater complexity and subtlety. Up till then there had been no strife between bourgeois social relations and productive forces, only a tension generating still greater fertility. But now this becomes dualism.

Formal logic is not a law of thought, it is a rule of symbolism. If we are to denote social references by social referents, if we are to indicate for social purposes socially interesting events in the flux of becoming by discrete, permanent symbols, there is one elementary necessity:

Each discrete permanent symbol must denote an entity on which our actions will converge.

For example if by 'this rock' we sometimes mean a tree, sometimes a cloud, there will be no social convergence. But a language is designed to secure social convergence. Hence 'this rock' must always secure social convergence.

This involves the so-called 'Laws of thought'. The Law of Contradiction, 'a thing cannot both be A and Not-A,' secures unidirection in social convergence. The Law of the Excluded Middle, 'a thing must be either A or Not-A,' secures unanimity in social convergence.

Logical laws are therefore social. They are approximate rules which must be obeyed if language is to fulfil a social function. They are in no way true of the nature of reality. They do not in fact make any statement about the nature of reality. They merely make the following statement:

'It is desirable to ensure co-operation in the active relation of society to reality.'

Of course this is tautologous, inasmuch as the existence of a language implies not merely the recognition of this law, but the fact that, even before language came into being, there must have been social co-operation to bring it into being. That is why logic is a late outgrowth from language.

Formal logic does not express the vital nature of reality, but expresses certain abstract characteristics of social action. Its laws are manifestly untrue as statements of reality. It is not true that a thing is either A or not A. Yesterday it was A; to-day it is not-A. It is not true that a thing cannot both be and not be A. To-day I am alive, some day I will be dead. To-morrow I will or will not be dead. Both alternatives are equally true. The use of the verb 'is' gives a spurious truth to the methodological rules of logic: it implies a universal instant; but this we know from relativity physics to be impossible. There is only a social instant. There is a 'present' common to members of society existing and moving at roughly the same speed and in the same place in the Universe and able therefore to undertake a co-operative task. Outside this society, the 'is' becomes a 'was' or 'will-be', and the 'laws' of logic cease to be valid. Even within society logic is only approximately true. It is a rough 'working' rule like the absolute Time and Space of conversation and appointment-making which is also an unreal social approximation.

Social tasks show us change in reality. Our symbols must be continually altered; our thoughts and forms continually become qualified and enriched. Our active contact with reality ensures a continual dialectical change in thought and perception, and the constant ingression of the new as the result of our changing relations with it. Thought therefore needs only to go out in action to remain dialectical; hence the dialectical nature of scientific hypotheses. The hypothesis goes out in the experiment and, as a 'result', becomes changed, and returns upon the hypothesis to alter it. The fresh hypothesis now gives rise to a fresh experiment. The experiment, if it negates the hypothesis, produces a new one, competent to synthesise both the negation and the original hypothesis.

Whenever we see thought becoming non-dialectical and logical, there must be a breach between thought and action. Instead of preoccupying itself with the changing subject-object relation, mind preoccupies itself with the forms of that symbolism which, in the past, has contained old dialectical formulations of realities. This indicates a similar process in society itself. The productive relations of society have become separated and antagonistic from the productive forces. The ruling class, the class whose philosophy language expresses, has ceased to be fertile, and has withdrawn and become merely parasitic. Thought has become introverted. We see this emphasis on logic, formalism, and withdrawal from action in the Hellenistic, Scholastic, and modern bourgeois philosophies. We see it in all developed philosophies, for the towering of philosophy as queen of thought is itself the reflection of a class cleavage. The development of logistic in contemporary thought is, like neo-realism, a good example of this trend. Logistic is a preoccupation not with the use of mathematics but with the nature of its symbolism. As a result logistic has not generated a single new development in mathematical thought.

Dialectics is not therefore—as the Scholastics imagined formal logic to be—a machine for extracting the nature of reality from thought. It is the denial of the possibility of the existence of such a machine. It is a recognition of mutually determining relations between knowing and being. It is a creed of action, a constant goad forcing the thinker into reality. Thought is knowing; the experience is being, and at each new step new experience negates old thought. Yet their tension causes an advance to a new hypothesis more inclusive than the old. When capitalism has generated at one pole, the exploited proletariat, with unprecedented misery, and at the other end, the exploiting bourgeoisie, with unprecedented wealth, a new quality emerges from their antagonism, that of Communism. A synthesis of the contradictions of bourgeois economy having come into being, these contradictions are now revealed nakedly as truth and error. Bourgeois philosophy now becomes sterile dualism, and it is proletarian philosophy or Marxism which is dialectic. But because it is the task of the proletariat, arising from the mode of their generation, to solve the problem of human relations and of the gulf between knowing and being, Marxism is more than a philosophy, it is a sociology. It is a theory of the concrete society in which philosophy, and other forms of ideology, are generated.

Bourgeois philosophy, therefore, can generate no greater philosophy than Hegel's, any more than feudalism could generate anything higher than Thomism or Hellenism anything more all-embracing than Platonism and Aristotelianism. To rise beyond Hegel's idealistic synthesis, one must see that the mind in its turn is determined by social relations, that knowing is a mutually determining relation between subject and object, that freedom is not accident but the consciousness of necessity. One must see that if freedom for a man in society is the attainment of individual desires, it involves conscious co-operation with others to obtain them, and that this conscious co-operation will itself transform a man's desires. To see this is to cease to be a bourgeois, and to cease to tolerate bourgeois economy. One is already a communist revolutionary. Bourgeois economy itself produces these, for to be shown that freedom does *not* lie in lack of social organisation is to be proletarianised. It is to be declassed, if one is a bourgeois or to be made class-conscious if one is a proletarian. It is to find how helpless one is by oneself to resist the dominating and exploiting relations that are concealed in bourgeois economy.

To have become a dialectical materialist is to have been subject to exploitation, want, war, anxiety, insecurity; to have had one's barest human needs denied or one's loved ones tormented or killed in the name of bourgeois liberty, and to have found that one's 'free-will' alone can do nothing at all, because one is more bound and crippled in bourgeois economy than a prisoner in a dungeon—and to have found that in this condition the only thing that can secure alleviation is co-operation with one's fellow men in the same dungeon, the world's exploited proletariat. This co-operation itself imposes on one's actions laws deriving from the nature of society and of the aims one has in common with those others. Then one has ceased to be a bourgeois philosopher: one has become a dialectical materialist. One has seen how men can leave the realm of necessity for that of freedom, not by becoming blind to necessity, or by denying its existence, but by becoming conscious of it.